Before I Get Old and Wrinkly!

by
Sheila Steptoe

Bloomington, IN Milton Keynes, UK

 authorHOUSE®

AuthorHouse™
1663 Liberty Drive, Suite 200
Bloomington, IN 47403
www.authorhouse.com
Phone: 1-800-839-8640

AuthorHouse™ UK Ltd.
500 Avebury Boulevard
Central Milton Keynes, MK9 2BE
www.authorhouse.co.uk
Phone: 08001974150

First published by AuthorHouse 7/25/2006

ISBN: 1-4208-2736-7 (sc)

All events are recorded to the best of the author's knowledge and recollection. The author takes full responsibility for their description. All opinions and recommendations are those of the author and no one else's.

Jacket cover by Michael Randall

Printed in the United States of America
Bloomington, Indiana

This book is printed on acid-free paper.

Authors details

Before I Get Old and Wrinkly is Sheila's first book which started as just a letter to her children but the idea and contents were beginning to help so many other people that she turned it into a book.

Her life has been an adventure and as a teenager in the late 60's early 70's Sheila and a group of girlfriends thumbed their way around Europe for 3 years, but she then settled down and was happily married for 20 years and had 2 children. They have now flown the nest and she now has beautiful grandchildren. She went back to work when her children were teenagers and having spent most of her working life at The Observer and Sunday Times newspaper went to work for her local newspaper. After 6 years she then trained to become a Health Care Adviser and the company thankfully took her away from sales and trained her 'in house' to be a trainer and teacher. She had found her vocation. She did a Counselling degree and trained to be a Life Coach before she took time out to write her letter. It has been a journey of self discovery.

Having had a corporate background in sales and been a volunteer for Victim Support Sheila decided to utilise her skills when writing her letter to her children. She has also written a second part within the book 'My thoughts on life'. This has now subsequently lead her on to a new successful business venture giving talks and running workshops to help others get the most out of their own lives. "I turned my letter into a book to make positive thinking more accessible to the general public, but there is no book, course or seminar that can actually change your life, until you yourself want to, but we can all learn something new". Her book is now making people think about their own lives and bringing people closer together.

Sheila lives in Essex and wrote the book in the comfort of her recently acquired 15th century cottage. She loves reading, learning, travelling and enjoying life to the full.

Dedication

This book is dedicated to:

My beautiful children Robert and Anni,
My beautiful grandchildren Simone and James
and any future grandchildren I may have

(I have changed their names for their privacy)

Acknowledgements

The first list of people I wanted to include here ran into pages - each name held a story in itself, each person had had an affect on my life, so much so, that a name was not enough. The support, encouragement, and the friendships of them all mean a great deal to me and I am sorry that I cannot include you all by name, but you know who you are.

I do have to say special thanks to a few people. To Janice, Theresa B, Mandy, Cathy T, Theresa S, Sharon N, for always being there and I could write pages on what you all mean to me.

To my long standing friends Molly, Sharon M, Greta, Karen, Tony C, Jenny and Del, Roger and Pat, who I have known since my teenage years and what wonderful friendships they have been and still are. As you will all know, there are too many others within our crowd to list here but we have all shared so much over the years.

To my friends Geoff, Anthony, Debbie, Fran, Cathy A, Rachel, Ginny and the new friends, who have recently joined us in Circle.

To my work colleagues who became friends over the last twelve years Julie, Sharon W, Derek, Lynn, and more recently Ray, Alan W, Colin B, Nigel, Rod, Peter who all encouraged me - it has been wonderful to work with you all. I can honestly say that to work with such lovely people has been a pleasure, and most of it was fun!

Also my friends Brenda, Clare, Doug, Lesley B, Jan H who showed me that life as single person is fun. Emma for her understanding, and Tony M for his support.

My editor, Lesley Townsend-White for her friendship and trust in me that this book was meant to be. Thank you.

I would also like to acknowledge some friends who have died quite young Wendy, Sheila, Les, Adonis and Anthony. And finally my mum, dad and ex-in-laws, who are all sadly missed.

Contents

Part Four

Book Two

Foreword

By the editor

When you pick up this book imagine the author to be in your sitting room with a cup of coffee (or more likely, a glass of red wine) and she is talking to you in a relaxed and informal manner, just as if she is your friend who has dropped by for a chat. The conversation rolls around various subjects – your work, your family, your relationships, and so on.

How Sheila would chat to you is the way she has recorded the words in her book, in an easy going manner. She wrote the book in just a couple of months. 74,000 words were tapped out with hardly a break from the keyboard, and she felt passionate about it. The book had been brewing for a number of years, but she had been wrestling with whether to publish or not. She was nervous, naturally enough, of exposing some quite intimate and emotional matters and who would be interested anyway? There is a natural curiosity about reading autobiographies of the famous but there is no real curiosity for the average person in the street to read about Sheila Steptoe. The one overwhelming need for her to publish was to help others....to give people a wake up call to get to know their family and friends on a deeper level and to do it NOW,

I read Book 1 in an evening and did wonder what the point of it was? Was it just an outpouring of troubles and woe describing a series of family events and arguments? I then read the contents of what is now Book 2 and saw the relationship between her life experiences and her thoughts on how she moved through each scenario.....separating out the emotions she went through and analysing them to herself as to why this and that happened. This I found constructive...and some of it I could relate to myself. The manuscript was untidy, well it was early days in the production of the book but she wanted my thoughts which I gave and then she threw in that she needed an editor.

It took me a minute to recall my past in publishing and I volunteered my services albeit having had no experience of editing an entire book. The red ball point quivered in my hand. (well to be more exact, my fingers hovered over the keyboard!) However, I restrained myself ......a perfectly written book was not the intention or in this case, important. What was important was its content and between us we discussed that to keep it, more or less, in its raw state gave it a certain appeal and Sheila wanted to keep its easy, chatty style. So here *I* was learning one of *my* lessons in life, learning to step back and go with the flow.

Towards the end of editing the final chapters I felt there was something missing. "Is there another reason for the book?" I asked. The answer came back weeks later because Sheila was still moving through her life's journey and getting to know herself. She decided it was "a closure for me on an unhappy period of my life which I cannot change at the moment and something I had to do in order to move on", she replied. There you have it. Everything is not solved for her but sometimes you have to let things rest to see how they unfold for themselves. This is what she has been prepared to do for the sake of, hopefully, saving the relationship with her daughter. Her distancing herself from the situation and getting on with other projects are not because she doesn't care, far from it.

Is she lucky to have found a way to close this particular episode of her life? Not lucky but forthright and hard working. She looked within herself and found a new belief and found the energy to move forward. Something she says any one of us can do when we need to.

There may be much you will be able to relate to your own life in this book. It is an aladdin's cave of emotions and the pearls and gems of wisdom are there for the taking. It is Sheila's intention that you *do* raid the cave for whatever you find useful. Most importantly she hopes to pass on the lessons she has learnt in her life so far to her children and grandchildren. Book 1 is written as a letter to them all. You might be shocked at being able to view her life in such a personal way and you may find it rambling, but if there is just a small section that gets you to question aspects of your life and spurs you into action to change what you are not happy with, then the book will have served its main purpose. To provide a wake-up call people might need in order to look "within" themselves to achieve happiness and to help them on their journey.

Some people are doing this already – looking inwards at themselves. They are turning away from money, possessions and other people to find the happiness they seek and are receptive to learning about the New Age - the Age of Aquarius[1] with its emphasis on humanity, kindness, truth, spirituality and enlightenment, all things that you can find within yourself. Sheila is definitely of the New Age.

Jonathan Cainer, astrologer for the Daily Mail, claims that 'the Age of Aquarius is truly dawning' and that 'the separate ancient Eastern and Western expectations are now dovetailing beautifully into one global vision of peace and hope.' Sheila's own vision is one of peace and hope. Her birth sign is also Aquarius so whether or not this has something to do with her spiritual awakening at this time, I don't know, and am not qualified to say. What I do understand is that her new belief in spiritualism has led her to her own self-improvement and that she has the potential to help others do the same. It has led her to writing this book which began as an inspiration, became a passion and which she turned into reality.

The weekend I was expecting to complete the final proof read, we actually put everything on hold due to emotional pressures Sheila was encountering. However, she held onto the main reason for the book which was to help others and she removed the "stop" and we moved onwards. "If it can help just one other family mend a rift between a grandparent and child or grandparent and grandchild then she will consider the book successful and worthwhile. Unfortunately similar situations are occurring in millions of other families - far too many".

In 1997 Prince Charles launched an initiative called Respect, which seeks to promote greater tolerance between faiths. He called for all religions to unite in 'faith in the integrity of life itself.' *Before I Get Old and Wrinkly* is not about religion and Sheila does not impose her beliefs on you. However, family turmoil expressed in her letter to her children and grandchildren does bring fighting and misunderstanding one another closer to home. It happens to most families. If we can teach respect and integrity to our children, generation to generation, it should spread naturally to the workplace and beyond into the world and may bring families and cultures together to live in harmony. We do not all have to be of the same religion, have the same interests, come from the same backgrounds to live in harmony. Respect for others, faith in ourselves and ownership of our actions are pieces in the jigsaw of life that will make things click together. This is all the author wants – togetherness, harmony in the family; harmony and peace in the world.

Let's hope she and we can achieve it.

Lesley Townsend-White

About my life and my journey to finding peace

Book One

My letter to you all

To my dear son, daughter and grandchildren,
    Where my life is going at this moment in time I am not quite sure but isn't life an exciting journey? It is full of so many different emotions and experiences that sometimes it is hard to put it into words. Everyone's life is like an adventure, each is different and personal, and sometimes we never know what will happen next. It can be full of magical moments, exciting and life can be great but then suddenly it can change in an instant. My life is like that and so much has happened that I felt I would like to write to you and tell you more about my life. You may wonder why and for what purpose but for various important reasons which I will explain to you as I write, I feel that the time is now right for you both and my grandchildren to know and understand the deeper me.

    Another reason to write to you now is that when nanny and granddad both died, I realised afterwards that I did not **really** know them, and in some ways that hurt and surprised me. It suddenly dawned on me – who were they? Why had I all my life just accepted that they were **just** my parents and I had never actually wanted or even thought about who they were as individual people? They had a life before I came along, but it never occurred to me to ask what it was like. Yes, I knew certain things but never knew their feelings, and all that they got up to! Both had done quite a lot in their lives, of which in some ways I knew very little. I am sure that they had a wonderful time, and that they were wonderful people... but it is too late for me to ask them now. The list of questions I needed answers to seemed odd in a way, as why did I not ask them when they were alive? Perhaps if I had, I would have felt differently after their death as I would have understood them more.

I also felt guilty in a way because mum and dad may not have known that I loved them? I never told them and I just assumed that they knew. We did not have the sort of relationship where loving words were said, or emotions expressed and I feel sad about that. That is why I tell you both often that 'I love you'. Those three little words are so hard for some people to say, but mean a lot.

At this moment you probably feel just the same about me now. I'm just your mum but I am also 'me'. I think this is normal. To you I may be old and beginning to get wrinkly but inside I am still young. I don't feel my age and according to one of you I don't act it either. What a lovely compliment it was when one of you said "mum I think you should grow up and stop acting like a teenager" but that is how I feel. I am sure I will be old one day but not yet.

I am having a lovely life with plenty of good times as well as bad, but since you all came into my life, I have never really been able to tell you how I have felt through various stages, as sometimes I find this hard. I think we may all be guilty of this, and perhaps we should talk more and then things might not get so muddled. But there never seems to be enough time. I have had a great life so far with some real fun and laughter. I have also had some real heart breaks, one of which is still breaking my heart today, as you know.

But before I met daddy, I had a life of which you know so little. I had a brilliant time. I grew up in the late 60's early 70's and that was a great era to be a teenager. We were the first to experience so many of the trends that you now copy! Mini skirts, platform shoes and so many of your modern songs are copies from my generation of song writers! The list is endless, but I also went through the

2

feeling that my parents never understood me - just like you felt when you were teenagers! I was your age once and did all the things you used to get up to! I also had boyfriends before I met daddy. A couple of them you know as we are still friends. And then when I met daddy, we had a brilliant marriage and for three years we had time together before the first one of you entered into our world. That really was such a wonderful honour to have you in our lives.

But of course, at the moment as you both know, the family is split apart through the most horrendous circumstances, and I have not been able to tell you how I have **really** felt. I never ever thought that one of you would ever do something as awful as this to me. No one can understand how I feel, unless they have experienced one of their children or grandchildren being taken away from them. I hope that this never happens to either of you, as the pain is **truly** unimaginable. The pain has eased with time, but the heartache nearly made me go insane. But what kept me sane were two things. My wonderful friends, who were brilliant, and something amazing that had started to happen to me. It is something which I have never ever really been able to explain to you properly, or even talk to you about, but it is beautiful. I will tell you about it as I write.

We have tried talking to each other but we did not seem to *hear* each other, so I hope that by understanding me better, and by writing about the experiences that have happened to us all, then in some way it may be easier to understand *why* it happened.

I am only writing about *my* feelings and thoughts, and how *I see* things. I am sure that you will both have your own feelings and thoughts on your own childhood and the experiences that we all have been through. There are always two sides to everything, but for some reason it is important to me that you may begin to understand me better, just as I had wanted to know and understand my own parents.

We all will never know each other completely, that would be impossible and I am sure that there may be lots in my life and yours, that we would **not** want each other to know. But I hope that you will begin to see why parents have 'unconditional love' for their children, no matter what happens. You both have children of your own, my grandchildren, whom I adore as you know. Hopefully I will have more grandchildren one day, and I am sure I will love them just as much as the two I have now. You also know that I will always love you both, but this circumstance I am afraid has caused me such pain that my heart has been broken.

But I also want my granddaughter to know that I have never ever forgotten her, and I never will. Not a day goes past without her being in my thoughts. I cannot begin to imagine the pain and hurt and the mixed emotions that she has gone through, at such a young tender age. I am sure we will see each other one day soon. I look forward to that day. Actually I am quite nervous about it, as I know that I will cry. But the tears will be tears of happiness, not sadness.

So let me start by telling you how I feel about my life and the emotions that I have now, as strangely enough through all the turmoil I have come to a stage when I now realize that I have inner peace. This is perhaps the secret to life, learning to find the peace within. It has taken me a long time to get to this wonderful stage and I am not quite there yet, being at *complete peace,* but I have learnt that through acceptance and faith that life does not have to be a struggle and we can learn to live in harmony.

Maturity .... arriving slightly creased

I love, I enjoy, I smile, I laugh, I feel, I weep, I cry, I hurt and I embrace but all with a big pain in my heart. This pain will not go away at the moment, but eases with time. But hey, what have I done to deserve such a mixture of emotions? Why do I feel such depth of pain that I never imagined possible? But through this, something so beautiful has also emerged, and has changed my whole being, that I now know why. I now have a sense of purpose. I now have passion; enthusiasm and vitality back in my life.

My life has been a real mixture of events, but by being positive throughout and looking within, I have been able to move on to being now at peace with myself, which is a lovely place to be. I know who I am, I like myself, and I am never alone, so never feel lonely. I now realise why I have been through a lot of these experiences. I now have the freedom **to be** who I am. Funny statement to make you may say, but I suddenly began, unbeknown to me at the time, a wonderful spiritual journey that has been truly amazing, and has kept me sane! It has helped me in many ways and given me more understanding about life. Now I am not asking you to think that you have to be a 'believer', or in anyway 'spiritual' to read this, because that it is not the purpose at all. I also have no intention of changing any of your ideas or beliefs if you are not open to them. The purpose is to help you to get to know who **you** really are as well, and to get to **know** the people who are in your life more deeply, and perhaps for you to start to realise how much they may mean to you, and how much you all mean to me. Also for you to understand that what ever happens in your life, it is how you learn to deal with things, and how you get through them, that is so important.

We each of us have a life which is unique. We all have different experiences, different pain and different pleasure but if by sharing with you some of my knowledge that I have gained over the years, then I hope that your eyes may be more open to the challenges of life. We are each travelling our own journey; we are all beautiful because we are all unique and special.

But, I have to start right at the beginning for you to understand who I am, and how I became the person that I am. This I hope will also help you understand why some of my most beautiful experiences have happened to me within my spiritual journey. I feel very honoured, privileged and in a way 'special'.

But, throughout my life, I tried not to ever feel bitter, resentful or why me? I could have done on quite a few occasions, but I had to move on with my life. Most people I am sure experience difficulties in some shape or form, but I hope yours will be minimal. With the help of some wonderful friends, I also have had some wonderful fun and laughter, which to me is so important. Laughter and love really are the basis of life I think, and to have both in your life is what we all deserve and I hope you will too

I hope it will help you to see that life is like a burning candle, and that sometimes when the flame goes out we can re-light it.

So let me explain as my life I now think has been divided into four parts. When I first realised this it surprised me that I looked at it in this way. It has been full of love, happiness, sadness, joy, tears, laughter, fun, trauma, cancer, deaths, divorce, and now a big separation, but always with deep friendships and love. I will explain as I go through my life, in some areas in brief detail only, as I could write about so much more in every area of my life, how through some amazing events, I have been exposed to the most profound emotions of peace, love and trust.

The first part of my life is my childhood and teenage years; the second part is my marriage and my children; the third part is my divorce and the time for ME, the fourth part is ME and others.

You may wonder why I put ME in capitals - well it is because as a mother, it took me so long to realise that I was ME again - not somebody else's attachment. Of course, I still am, and always will be, your mum and nan, and daddy's ex-wife, but I now have another identity - myself, which took me a long time not to feel guilty about.

Part One

My youth .... embroidered with adventure

Now this part of my life really is different to what followed later, as in my childhood and teenage years, I had such a wonderful time. Nothing really unhappy happened so when events much later in my life started, I really was shocked. Until then, I thought that I was one of the privileged and nothing bad was ever going to happen. I somehow drifted through life and took nothing too seriously. I am the eldest of four girls. We were all born into a quite well-to-do family, with well-respected parents. We loved them but we were not close. It was not a family that kissed each other or told each other everything and we all felt that we could not approach mum and dad in the sense that we could tell them all that we were getting up to. We just somehow learnt to get on with it, but in some ways that was quite good as we all grew up being individual, independent adults with no major hang ups. Mum and dad played golf a lot and we were brought up with a variety of foreign au pairs. Some of these girls were lovely, but I am afraid that some we did not like at all and, if I remember correctly, my sisters and I were not very nice to one or two of them!

I never heard my parents raise their voice, argue, get angry or cross or even swear and they were very happy. My dad never ever smacked us – that was left to mum!

We did all the normal things you do in a family like visit relatives, had family outings, Brownies, piano lessons, choir on a Sunday, ballet classes, playing tennis as our house had a tennis court. We went ice skating, roller skating in the street and had a couple of pets. We used to dress them up in clothes and parade them around in our dolls pram! We also went to fancy dress parties at the Mansion House every year, and my dad was once in the Lord Mayors show. I can remember watching him ride passed in a splendid carriage. He used to take us to his office every Saturday morning which for some reason was a real treat for us. I also remember mum and dad entertaining quite a lot and we used to watch silently from the top of the stairs in awe.

We went to the same seaside holiday place, in the summer school holidays, for years. We always rented a beach hut and we later took you there when you were both children. As we got older, mum and dad took us on various holidays to Scotland, and we went ski-ing in Aviemore. We also went on a cruise to the Mediterranean and Norway. I remember going to visit my mum's castle in Scotland called Brodie Castle, as this was her maiden name which became a family joke. I also remember going to visit my uncle's grave as my dad's brother, Uncle Willie, died very young, (aged 18) in action at the end of the First World War. This had affected dad throughout his life, and he cried at the grave. My sisters and I have never forgotten that.

Robert, you have grandad's brother's medals and personal possessions that he gave to you and I hope that you will always treasure them.

My dad had a successful accountancy business and was a chief magistrate. He was a fair and quiet man who never wanted a fuss made and hated any sort of violence. He had done a lot with his life before he met my mum. He was raised in Motherwell near Glasgow in Scotland but came down to England when he was 6. Although, strangely enough he always considered himself Scottish! Before he married, he had travelled a lot and went to work in Venezuela during the time of the Prohibition, and I would have really loved to have known more about that. That must have been so adventurous and dangerous and exciting. In the war he joined the Home Guards and was very proud of it, and he then met my mum at a tennis club just after the war. But did he have girlfriends before her? No idea as I never asked. What was his childhood like and how did he manage to build such a successful business? How did he feel during the war, and when his life was suddenly turned around when they moved to England?

My mum was 13 years younger than him, and she had worked in a bank for most of her life, like her own father who was a bank manager, your great grandfather. She had two sisters who I think she was quite close to. She joined The Women's Land Army and drove an ambulance during the war in Basingstoke. What were her experiences during this time, and again, what did she get up to before and during the war, before she met dad? What did she do and how did she feel on VE day? Why was dad so different to her other boyfriends? How did she feel when she saw him for the first time? Was it love at first site or did they get to know each other as friends first?

All these things I just took for granted and somehow never really asked, but I wish now I had. I am sure there were lots of things in both their lives that they may not have wanted us to know, as we can never know anyone completely, but I would have loved to have known more about their adventures especially in their own childhoods and school days. I also do not remember much about either of my grandmothers as they both died when I was a child. I do have vague memories of them but nothing I am afraid that stands out. I never knew either of my grandfathers as they died before I was born, and I feel sad that I never knew them. They are part of our family history. My sisters seem to know a lot more about our family and all the relations than I do, but I was not interested at that time. Now I am so it is nice to learn more from them.

A few years ago, strangely enough, I asked my sisters what they remembered about our childhood and it was really quite interesting as we all remember differently. How is this possible as we all came from the same parents?

Perhaps you feel the same too, but we tried to bring you up as equals, the same as my parents did. We always tried to treat you the same and be fair which is a big lesson I learnt from my parents. My youngest sister, Maryanne, remembers mum and dad as very loving – I cannot remember once sitting on my mum's lap but she can. I am not saying that I did not feel my mum's love, but maybe Maryanne was more open with my mum. She remembers telling mum and dad lots of things I would never have dreamt of telling them! How strange. My sister Liz had similar memories to me, but one thing she did say was that, probably I could not remember much about our childhood as nothing much extraordinary or unusual happened.

But one thing we all agreed on was that we knew we were loved as we loved mum and dad, and that they were always there for us, no matter what, and just wanted us to be happy. Somehow they were never judgmental of us, only if we did things seriously wrong would they say they were disappointed in us, which actually in some ways was more powerful. We were never told off for not being top of the class as long as we did our best. Our happiness, and for each of us to grow up as individual, independent people feeling secure was more important to them. I learnt a lot from my childhood and I hope that you have the same feelings about me and daddy. All we ever asked of you was just to do the best in all areas of your life that you can. But also that you did not have to be top of the class. As long as you were kind, thoughtful, understanding and true to yourself and others then I hope we have been as successful parents as my parents were. We tried to instil in you values and guidance that I hope you can pass on to your own children. One thing that I have learnt is that we are all individual people, so I tried to let you be you. We all make mistakes throughout life as sometimes this is how we learn and we all have different experiences, but I hope that you will begin to see that if you are true to yourself and you lead your own life as the person that you are, then you will learn from your own lessons and grow into contented adults.

There are two things that really stand out in my earlier years. One is that at the age of 10 I had a road traffic accident; a van knocked me off my bike when I was riding home from school, and I fractured my skull and put my spine out of place. This affected my back for most of my life, but is fine now. When I came home from hospital my sisters ran away from me and would not sleep with me because I had two big black eyes! The other thing which did affect me was that I was sent to boarding school at the age of 11 and I hated it. My mum had previously taken me to London to get my school uniform and then a few days later, took me to one of the big London train stations and put me on a train with a load of strangers and said "bye dear, see you soon" and just walked away. I honestly had no idea where I was going or why, but I have never forgotten it either. It turned out to be a school in Bedford. I am afraid that I rebelled, and a couple of years later I got expelled, so my parents sent me and my two sisters to another school. This time in Clacton, but I didn't take any notice of being told I couldn't listen to my radio at night under my covers as I wanted to listen to Radio Caroline which was all the rage (my friends at home did so why couldn't I?) so the teachers said I had to go. So, again I got expelled. Actually, it was not just for that, but to me life at school was far more interesting if you had fun. I was not the most academic in my class but I did exceed at sport. I loved sport and was good at it and often in the school sports lacrosse and hockey teams. But through my bad experiences at school, I never wanted either of you to go to boarding school, as I wanted you to share your school life with us.

My parents then sent me to a local college to learn secretarial skills, but I talked too much, so after the first term I was asked to leave. God, my parents must have despaired but I must say were very good. Do you know I have never actually put on my CV that I got expelled from two schools, asked to leave from college and never taken an exam as my trunk was packed for me before I could! It has never ever stopped me getting any job that I have wanted. But after leaving college, mum and dad then found me a job in the West End Department Store, Debenham and Freebody, and I thrived. I loved it and was promoted time and time again. I then got a job on The

11

Observer Newspaper and I was starting to meet some fabulous people who were exciting.

I was also going out to the coffee bars with a group of girlfriends, some of whom are still my friends today. It was in the time of the mods and rockers and we had a whale of a time. All the guys had scooters as I was a mod and we used to go away for weekends down to the coast sometimes and it was great. We then ventured to the clubs, locally and in London, and started to drink alcohol and we did see some groups who became very famous later on. The Who, Small Faces, Otis Reading, Ike and Tina Turner, Georgie Fame and such people. The late 60's was really a brilliant time to be a teenager. We all had such fun and we were, in some ways, so innocent, and all we wanted to do was enjoy life, and we did. It was also a time when, as I said earlier, I felt that mum and dad did not understand me and to me going out and enjoying myself was what teenage life was all about. I could actually write so much more about this time and how I felt because I do understand how exciting our teenage years are, and maybe when your children are teenagers you will understand why ground rules are put in place! It isn't until we have our own children that this makes sense!

At the age of 17, I was the first of our group of girls to pass my driving test and I used to borrow my mum's car which was a Morris Minor Traveller and we went everywhere in it. But, we were hard-up in those days so bought alcohol to drink before we went to the clubs and my friends used to hand me a glass whilst I was driving. When you think about it; I am afraid to say that that was *very* wrong. There was me, driving with my girlfriends in the back, with a glass of Merrydown (a sort of wine) in my hand!

My mum and dad's house was open house to my friends and they were always popping round for coffee and listening to records as we had our own front room which mum and dad never came into. I also had loads of brilliant parties when they went away for weekends with my younger sisters. Some of the damage that was done was always noticed by my mum. At the time I thought that we had tidied up well, but if anything got broken my friends always had a whip round to pay for the damage. I can relate to that Yellow Pages advert with drawings on a painting, as I often had to look up someone to come to the rescue. Two incidents stand out because to get a leaded light specialist on a Sunday morning is not easy, as a window had been broken. Another time was when one of the boys, John, decided to be Tarzan and swung on a chandelier at the bottom of the stairs and the light came out of the ceiling, just as mum and dad were coming home! No wonder I was the black sheep of the family, but I did not worry about that, as I was far more interested in enjoying my teenage years. Oh, the times my dad called the police because I had not come home on time. But hey, what is time when you are enjoying yourself! Now you may realise why I was not keen for you to have parties at our family home when we went out! I hope we never stopped you enjoying yourself but my home was precious to me and I knew what you may have got up to as I did. A lot of my friends in my teenage years are still friends today and we still remember those good times. I have always been very lucky with my friends and I think it is important to keep in touch.

When I was 19 a group of girlfriends and I decided that we wanted to travel the world, so we packed our bags and off we went. In the late 1960's this was very adventurous and not something a lot of teenagers did. We thumbed our way right down to Benidorm which was THE up and coming place in those days. We all had such a wonderful time, but we were very sensible. Actually there were six girls and we all got on so well which is quite an achievement and five of us are still friends. Michelle moved away so we lost touch, but you know the others Karen, Greta, Jenny and Gill. We stayed and worked there for six months, and when we came back, one of the girls Karen and I had real itchy feet. So after two weeks at home, we packed our rucksacks and off we went. This time we went to Holland, and do you know we took part in Amsterdam's history. We were at the first students' rebellion in Dam Square in the early 70's and it is actually recorded there now but was a very frightening experience for us. It was unheard of to have riot police on horseback then, and I don't think I have ever run so fast in my life. Then, we went on to other European countries where we again thumbed and worked, and in all that time we had no other major trouble. I am afraid that would not be the case today as it would be so much more dangerous. We worked in various places, and then we travelled back to Benidorm as we felt at home there and Karen had fallen in love the previous year so wanted to see her boyfriend, whom she later married. Again we were away for about six months and when we came back, another group of my girlfriends wanted to do the same, so asked me if I wanted to work in the Canary Islands with them, so off I went. This time it was with Molly, Sharon and Greta. But this time I did not like it as much, but got a job cooking for a group of English taxi drivers which was fun, but we all decided after 3 months to go back again to Benidorm which we did. We all stayed and had a brilliant time, and I got a job in one of the top nightclubs selling hamburgers, which was great. You can actually make a lot of money when people are drunk and hungry! That really was one of the cream jobs but I decided that I had had enough so came home after 10 months, and my life was about to take a completely different turn. Because of the wonderful experience of my travels and the fun that we had, when you, Robert, wanted to travel to Australia and work at about the same age as me, I gave my blessing. It really was a wonderful experience and something that I am so pleased that we both did.

A few days of being at home, two friends Tony and Karen suggested and arranged for me to meet an acquaintance of theirs who they thought I would get on with. They were right and 10 days later he asked me to marry him, so that was the end of my travels and another journey was about to begin.

Part Two

My thirties ... zipping along, married and a mum

We got married in February 1973, and I was just 24. We bought a very old cottage in the country, quite a distance away from where I grew up. We did it up with the help of my wonderful in-laws and some builder friends. It needed major renovation and it even had an outside toilet in a shed! It was one year and a day after we married that we finally moved in. We did not have much furniture but it was heaven. We had a bed, which was a wedding present, one table and four chairs, a cooker and daddy fixed up a pole for our clothes. We had nothing else but we did not care. In fact, on the evening we moved in, we had to take all nine stairs out to get the bed up to the bedroom, as cottages have such small staircases. Until they could be repaired, we had to climb up to bed on a ladder! We had lived with my mum and dad for a year and one day and that was great. But there is no place like your own. We gradually saved and furnished the place, and Robert you were born there two years later. Daddy had his own transport business and things were great. We were very happy there and loved our cottage. We had so many animals I forget how many, but they included dogs, goats, chickens, rabbits and a horse.

After five years, we decided to move to a bigger house but daddy's business then folded, not the best timing but we continued with the move and this was to become your family home which you loved. Then, I was pregnant again, along with two of our dogs Flossie and Sasha who had eight puppies on the day we moved in. Again, this was a house to renovate which we did over the next few years. It was a large Victorian Grade II listed house with an acre of ground, in a small village near to our old cottage. We extended the property with a new kitchen and bathroom, and added three stables for the horses we planned to buy when you were older. It also had a cellar which daddy converted, with the help of my brother-in-law, Uncle Bob, into an area for a train set, which took up the whole cellar floor. I am sure you will remember that. The men and your friends used to spend many hours down there. Anni, you were born a few months after the move and everything was wonderful. We did have such lovely times there with you both growing up, as I am sure you will remember. Before we did any of the renovations, we had a big party for all of our friends, but the kitchen was quite small, and had a second bathroom next to it. People were actually standing in the bath in order not to miss any of the action. Why is it that everyone always wants to congregate in the kitchen at parties?

Another beautiful party we had at this house, but quite a few years later, was for my dad's 80th. My dad was Scottish and loved the bagpipes, and was always talking about Robbie Burns and everything to do with being Scottish, so we organised a big surprise for him. We got together all the family, my dad's business partners and a lot of his friends, and had lunch out on the lawn. The day was beautiful. As we were having lunch, one of our friends John, who played the bagpipes, had organised for three of his colleagues and himself to march into our garden unannounced, playing a very famous Scottish tune. The look on my dad's face was beautiful, and the surprise on the guests' faces was brilliant. We hadn't told anyone but everyone there knew what the bagpipes meant to my dad. I don't think there was a dry eye at the party. He was in his element, and just grinned from ear to ear, and after they played quite a few tunes, my dad took a whiskey to each of them, and thanked them. Then they played a tune with my dad standing in the middle, and then started to march out of the garden. My dad just stepped into line and proceeded to march out with them. He loved it so much that John agreed to come back with a full band and play again for his 90th, but unfortunately dad died aged 88. How he would have loved that. I cannot hear the bagpipes even to this day without tears welling up in my eyes. I was never a great lover of them, but I can understand how moved people must have been, when they heard them over the hills. We took a video of this party for us all to keep the memory.

Just before this party and when Anni you were three, along with some friends we all went on our first holiday abroad to Sardinia. Unfortunately, you had an epileptic fit in the middle of the night and the hospitals in Italy in those days left a lot to be desired. We were told you were brain damaged as the fit went on for nearly an hour, so we had to fly home straight away. Robert, do you remember the pilot let you fly in the cockpit with him and you landed the plane at Heathrow because it was your birthday and we were the only people on the flight? Anni you being ill really was a shock. We went to Great Ormond Street hospital and the specialist was brilliant and said it was a feberal convulsion due to a high temperature, and a middle ear infection. Unfortunately you started having more fits, but always in the middle of the night so you slept in our bedroom until you were ten. Fortunately you were a very heavy sleeper! I felt very guilty for a long, long time afterwards that if I had not wrapped you up in a blanket when the fit started, perhaps you would not have had any more fits, but in those days Epilepsy was not talked about so I had no idea I was doing wrong. Epilepsy was a taboo subject, but fortunately today there is no stigma, and children and parents know much more about what to do[2]. You fortunately grew out of the fits by the age of 10.

So, because of our experience and the trauma that it caused, we decided that we could not take a chance of going abroad again and we bought a caravan. A few of our friends had got one, so nearly every weekend in the summer for quite a few years, on a Friday night, what ever the weather, I would pack up the van with food and alcohol.

17

Daddy would arrive home from work, hook the van up and off we would go and meet our friends and yours, and we had some great times. We would then pack up on a Sunday night and go back home. We had campfires in the evenings in the New Forest, where the ponies used to just walk into the awnings in the morning. Sometimes the barbeques were under umbrellas as we never knew what the English weather would be like. Other times it would be long weekends locally, usually only about an hour away by car, and it was great. I know that you both thoroughly enjoyed it. We even took the van to Spain and France with friends, and the freedom it gave the family was wonderful.

Appreciating life

Then, in September 1984, when you were both very young, I discovered a mole on my left arm had turned 'funny' and my doctor immediately sent me to a specialist who did a biopsy and told me it was skin cancer and operated straight away. I can't tell you the feeling you have when a doctor says to you "It is Cancer". It is something that you think will never happen to you as it only happens to others. It's as scary as hell. I think it is the fear of the unknown which is the hardest bit. But for some reason I could not acknowledge some of the thoughts and feelings that I got. Will I die? Will I survive? Will it hurt? Will I cry? Has it gone anywhere else? How will you all manage without me? I can still remember some of the thoughts that went though my head when first told, but I tried to push most of them to one side.

He did an 'envelope' operation on my arm which I am so grateful for. Normally the cancer is just dug out and is covered with a skin graft, so you have a massive hole. I was also very fortunate to have private medical insurance, and both these factors, I believe, saved my life. Three other friends in the same month had the same diagnosis but one unfortunately died a little while later. I have since discovered that one in three people die from it. Actually, he died a few years later on the same day I had another cancer scare when I discovered a lump in my breast. The skin cancer had obviously been due to my years of travelling and lying on the beach all day, but in those days too much sun causing skin cancer was not advertised as much as it is now.

Anyway, I decided that there was no way I was going to dwell on this. I was still in my thirties, I had two young children and I decided I would just get on with it. To me, there was no other way to deal with it. I was very fortunate and did not have to have chemotherapy, as my doctor had hopefully removed all the cancer. But there is always a possibility that he had not got it all out, so I tried to put that thought to the back of my mind. It seemed the only way I could deal with it, and never really spoke to anyone including daddy about how I felt. I just had to be strong. I was checked every three months for a long time, and I decided that if the cancer had travelled further to my lymph glands or elsewhere, I would deal with it then. I could not see the point in worrying about something that might not happen. I have since had a lot of moles removed as a precaution, because they had changed shape and if not removed would turn into cancer. But I have always had a positive attitude and I had the same approach to the news that I had a lump in my bust, which when operated on fortunately turned out to be non malignant. Being told you may have cancer a second time is a very scary feeling. I had to wait quite a few days to see the specialist and the waiting for the results was traumatic, but this time I was lucky.

Then there was a scar on my lung (from pneumonia I had suffered from years ago fortunately). But then, to top it all I had a fall in the garden when everyone's nightmare happened to me - I lost my two front teeth. Not a pretty sight I assure you, a lady with no front teeth! Fortunately I found a dentist, who has since become a friend, who made me a wonderful set of dentures that did not make me gag. The first set on the NHS were awful and how anyone puts them in their mouth without gagging I am not sure. All these events were beginning to teach me that life sometimes throws things at you that you never expect but by not dwelling on the negative side, and thinking positively I could be strong and I was. To me that is my way of coping and I have found that strength is part of my character. We are not all strong so if you find yourself at a difficult time in your life, and you can be strong then hopefully you will get through it. We each have to deal with our own experiences in our own way. I have learnt that feeling sorry for myself was not going to get me anywhere, and felt that these were part of my life's challenges and I am sure you will all have your own to deal with later in life, because that is part of life. So, if you can try to be positive at all times, then you can move on without struggling so much. If you can just 'accept' them and somehow be strong then you will develop strength.

Next obstacle - education

I think having a positive attitude to all of my scares, and misfortunes, and not dwelling on the negative side of it helped me and the family to continue life as normal. Life was good, you were growing up fast, but Anni you were having difficulty at school and this caused quite a lot of problems. Because of your epilepsy, your fellow pupils and teachers considered you 'different'. You had a form of epilepsy called *status epilepticus*, which means that you would have one convulsion after another unless brought out of it, usually by a suppository. You both went to the local village school, and the teachers there were brilliant. But you at this time also had a hearing problem, caused by continuous ear infections, and it was also discovered that you were severely dyslexic. I am afraid that your infant form teacher was not the most patient with you. She used to call you 'thick and stupid', which had an enormous effect on you for the rest of your life. Dyslexia does not mean that anyone is 'thick' and often children with dyslexia have an above average IQ. You and many others have other gifts, possibly with their hands as we later were to discover with you, or musically, but thankfully nowadays, dyslexia is much more recognised and the children can get much needed help[3]. One of the things that did help you Anni, was the pink glasses an optician recommended you to wear.

Because you had to have a valium type suppository inserted whenever you had a convulsion, and what with your dyslexia, and other slight learning difficulties, the education authorities wanted to send you to a special needs school. What a battle we were then about to encounter and we had a difficult decision to make. Your were on the border line as to whether you would have benefited from attending such a school. To them it would have been much easier and better for you, but we felt differently. We did look at a couple of the local special needs schools, which were brilliant for the children that needed them. These children thrive, but we felt that some children were not as socially mature as you. You were a very sociable child and we felt that it was best to keep you in a mainstream environment where your social skills could be developed. We also took advice from The Dyslexic Institute and a couple of educational psychologists, and we also paid for a dyslexic tutor to help you at home, who was a lovely lady but that was not enough for the education authorities. You were 'statemented' so that hopefully you could be given the much needed help that daddy and I knew you needed.

But events that followed were devastating. We were told, a few months later after you had been statemented, one Friday night, by one new young social worker, that if we objected to them sending you to a special needs school, which they wanted to do, they could take you into care and we would have no say over the matter. Well, how dare they! What an awful weekend that was. Here was this new social worker, who had never even met you, but was assigned to you because of maternity leave taken by the one social worker who knew and understood you, saying they would take you into care. So, we felt we had no alternative and we made the decision to send you to a private school but we also started to look into special schools that could cater for children with dyslexia. We visited quite a few in Suffolk and Norfolk who have some brilliant schools that would have been wonderful for you, but we could not afford to pay the fees. They were expensive, but we managed to find a private local day school. We also decided that our only alternative was now to take the education authority to court to fight for your rights. Well, we did and we won but it took 7 years; by that time, you were nearly at school leaving age. You had gone back into the main stream of schools at the age of 11 which was what you wanted to do, but unfortunately you were not given all the special help that you needed and got expelled.

So now you had home tuition by a lovely lady who agreed with us, that a special needs school would not have been appropriate. After we won, you got a place at another local comprehensive which was brilliant and I had wished that we had sent you there years ago. You stayed up to your final year, and I think made more progress in that year, than you did in the whole of your school life. You then went out into the big wide world of employment, but I am afraid that was a different story. You found it very hard to cope, could not read or write properly but your home tutor had discovered that you were brilliant at sewing, like your grandmother, and you made some wonderful quilts. For someone of 15, these quilts were beautiful. You made the first one for your brother for his 18th and it was lovely. Lots of it done by machine and hand, and you really should have pursued that line of work. I still have it at home. But no, I am afraid that you rebelled against a lot of jobs that you had, and were far more interested in socialising with your friends, and actually never lasted long in any job that you had.

Our social life

Daddy's transport company was doing well and we were living a good life. We were both in our thirties and having fun. A lot of our social life at this time seemed to revolve around the local village school, which put on some wonderful social evenings, and probably some of the best were the barn dances. Well, they were even better if you were pissed, as this creates so much more fun, as you don't hurt yourself when you fall over! They were always held at the local riding school, so we used to sit on bales of straw, true to traditional barn dances, and a lot of our friends would come, as well as the local friends from the school, because we used to have such a laugh. All the children would also participate, but I think you all got more fun out of watching your parents make a fool of themselves on the dance floor. Another event that the school would put on was not available to you or your friends. This was adults only! These were brilliant evenings at Christmas time, as one of the dads was in quite a famous band, and they would come and play every year, along with a famous comedian, and oh what a laugh we had. Somehow I would usually try and hide myself, so that I would not be picked out to be ridiculed, as they like to do, but they found me! Why is it always the ones that don't want to be picked, that they pick on. They really were good fun, and an event that we all used to look forward to. One of the dads also used to run the local pub, and Chris and Linda were wonderful and put on some brilliant fund raising events as well. Another event that stands out in my mind is the children's sports day. Nothing unusual about that you may say as all children have sports days, but there was one child attending the school who had a disability and was in a wheelchair. But, she was never left out which was wonderful. They used to create a special race for her, where the headmaster himself and a few other children would have a roly-poly race, and they would roll to the finishing line, and I think that was wonderful. Village schools do seem to have a small friendly atmosphere, which I think benefited you both. When Robert you first attended, there were only about 35 children in the whole school, and you cannot get better attention than that. Long waiting lists soon appeared, but the school to this day is still thriving.

Robert when you left school you went to the local agriculture college to follow your dream of working on a farm. You loved it, and had got a job on a local farm, and you thoroughly enjoyed looking after the animals, driving the tractors etc, and were in your element. You were very fit in those days, and used to cycle to work, and even got stopped by the local policeman for speeding on your bike. You were doing over 30mph and that was not even down a hill! You also, at this time, joined Young Farmers, which is a brilliant social organisation, who interact with other branches throughout the country. You participated in all the activities and were even Mr. Chelmsford one year, participated in the tug of war team, and with your training, you could watch your thigh muscles grow by the day, but you were thriving. You had learnt to drive and saved up yourself for your first car, a Mini. It was modified of course. You also seemed to be getting a lot of attention from girlfriends, and doing all the normal things that teenagers do. Do you remember, you had on your 18th birthday a few years later a brilliant party in a barn of the parents of one of your young farmer friends, and they all certainly know how to enjoy themselves? But, they all seem to consume a lot of alcohol and actually one of your friends Greenie died in his teens at a Young Farmers gathering which was a tragedy. Actually you have lost a couple of friends in their prime. Charlie was another friend who died in a tragic accident. So sad.

When you were both young, and Anni, you were having convulsions at school, I had chosen to stay at home, so that I could be on hand if needed, but I also decided to turn the spare room into a little business selling second hand clothes, which was brilliant. All my friends and the local mums would come and exchange their children's and adults' unwanted clothes, for clothes that I had displayed on the rails. I don't think I ever paid full money for any of your clothes for years, as nanny my mother-in-law also made clothes for you, so the little shop was a winner all round. Except, daddy used to get cross because it turned out to be a mothers' meeting place and friends would stay till quite late, chatting of course, and he used to get cross because I was not earning any money really. It gave me a role and my own identity and I enjoyed it. When you both got a bit older, I decided to return to work and got myself a part-time job on the local paper in advertising which I was thrilled about. I got the first job I had applied for after so many years and I can remember buying daddy a lovely present for Christmas out of my first three months wages and that gave me so much pleasure. Our family life was good and we did so many fun things together. We were a very close family and life just plodded on as normal. Well, as normal as it can be bringing up children, but nothing too drastic other than Anni your epilepsy and your problems at school, which really did affect you and thinking back I think the whole family.

Family bereavements

Then, a few years later in 1990, completely out of the blue, granddad my father-in-law, George, had a stroke, which left him unable to speak and nanny my mother-in-law, Gladys, had to do everything for him, including talking for him. We had planned for their Golden Wedding Anniversary a big surprise party but due to George being unwell, took them away for a lovely weekend break instead. They were a lovely couple who were very close to us all and you both had a very special bond with them.

Unfortunately, granddad being ill took a lot out of nanny and on Mothers' Day six months later; we were going to take them out for lunch when nanny phoned to say she did not feel well. So we went over to their house only to find her in a bad way with pains in her chest, so we called an ambulance and she was rushed to hospital, where we were told that she had had a small heart attack, but was ok. After a few hours we went home to get some things for her, but unfortunately she had another heart attack, and died before we got back. That was a real shock and it left us all numb. She was the first close relative that we had all lost, and we missed her enormously. It was strange to think that she would not be around anymore. Actually, we all felt the loss in different ways and I can remember saying to daddy that I knew how he felt as I was very close to her, and he said "no you don't" and I was hurt at the time, but I later learnt that that statement was true. It wasn't until my own father died that I knew what he meant. It is the emptiness and feeling so alone that is difficult to describe, and unless you have felt it, then we can only sympathise.

Granddad, my father-in-law, could obviously not look after himself so he came to live with us. I am sure you will remember that. As I said, I had got a job by this time on a local newspaper, only part-time, but I loved it but had to give it up to look after George. That was difficult as he was like a child, and looking back it did put a strain on our marriage. But we tried to be compassionate with him and did the best we could at the time. Do you remember how annoyed you both used to get when he would keep playing with the remote control to the television and you could not watch the programmes that you wanted to? When you were ill, strangely enough it brought daddy and me closer. When a child is ill, it either brings you closer or splits you apart. Unless you have had an ill child, it is difficult to understand the strain it puts you under.

The holiday and then .....

Then at the beginning of 1992 Daddy got a big tax rebate from the Inland Revenue, so in April we decided to visit my sister and friends in Australia, as Anni you had stopped having convulsions and you were both older by then. We had to find George a nice nursing home while we were away so that he was well looked after, which we did, and then off we went for six brilliant weeks. We stopped over in the Far East in Bangkok and Hong Kong, and then went to Perth to my sister and spent a few weeks with her and Uncle Bob and your two cousins. They had made a decision to move to Australia about six years previously, so it was a lovely reunion. Then we flew to Sydney to meet up with an old friend Tony, who was renting a house over looking Sydney Harbour, and just outside his house there were approximately 50 steps down to his own little beach - excuse me! Do you remember he hired a small boat and took us on a boat trip on Sydney's river by the harbour?

Then we went on to Brisbane to see some other friends, my old travelling friend Jenny and her husband Del, Barry and Rosemary, and an old school friend of daddy's and his wife. We spent a lovely couple of weeks with them all, having barbeques and drinking around their pools, oh what a life they have. We also spent a few days in their holiday resort of Noosa, which is THE place to be seen and I personally think has much better surfing waves than Bondi Beach, which we had previously visited. Perhaps we just saw Bondi on a calm day. Then the last few days we spent in Cairns, where we all went White Water Rafting

- wow, what an experience and not for the faint hearted but a very enjoyable experience! I must say that I was also very frightened. Then we went deep-sea diving in the Barrier Reef, which is out of this world, horse riding on a ranch, and please bear in mind daddy and you both were very competent riders, and I had not been on a horse since our honeymoon in 1973. The ranches were large, and I mean large, and after about four hours in the saddle before a break for lunch, I can assure you I could hardly walk. Actually I had borrowed one of your new pairs of jeans which did not fit properly. When you all saddled up for the afternoon ride, I strangely enough declined. You all loved it, but I loved a soft hammock in the sun better that afternoon, and then finally a visit to the Rain Forest which ended a wonderful, wonderful holiday. We really did enjoy it and it was a great experience as I am sure you will both agree.

When we got back, unfortunately daddy's firm started to get into difficulty, and such a lot had happened to daddy over the last year, and this was in some ways the beginning of the change in him. His dad had had a stroke but had gone back home to live, and his mother had died suddenly, all within one year and because of the toll of all these events, it was about to change our lives, as other tragedies were about to happen.

In August 1992, one year after my mother-in-law had died, my father became ill and the hospital could not find out what was wrong with him. So we rang my sister in Australia who said she would come home in a couple of months, as we did not realise how serious it was - nothing was going to happen to our dad! But we had to ring her back to say come quickly as he had taken a turn for the worse. So my sister booked a flight home, and my dad went into a coma, but she arrived just in time, and sat by my dad's bed, where she took his hand and he squeezed it, and he then died peacefully a couple of hours later. It was as though in a coma, he had waited for Maryanne to be there, and died peacefully knowing that all his family was around him.

What a strange, horrible feeling it is when a parent dies. It leaves you numb and somehow helpless and lost.

Your world is suddenly turned upside down, and you can walk along the street trying to carry on as 'normal' and see people laughing and joking and you feel like saying to them - "hey, do you know what has just happened to me - I am sad?" However time does heal, and somehow we carry on and we get through it. I remember crashing the car the day after dad had died as my concentration was shot to pieces. Somehow you go on 'auto-pilot' and just function. It takes years for the pain and tears to go away, and for a long time I could not talk about my dad without tears welling up in my eyes.

Part Three

My Forties .... ripped apart

Somehow life carries on, and there are many days when you can be 'normal' and then there are other days when you cannot stop the tears flowing. It just happens. Something or someone can say something and the floodgates just open. We each deal with it in our own way. Apart from the sadness from the loss of my mother-in-law, and the recent death of my dad, life was good. Daddy had a transport business, which had been very successful, I had got the first job I applied for after 10 years of being at home (although I had run my own second hand clothes business from home when you both were younger) and we had a very good social life. We had three babysitters in the village so we could alternate and go out either on a Friday night or a Saturday which we considered 'our' time and we did an awful lot with you both. Daddy and you all loved riding and we had three horses, plus other animals and for daddy's 40th birthday I had given him 'horse carriage driving lessons' which was something he had always wanted to do. All three of you also used to go hunting, and there was a very good social life - it kept you both off the streets as you had a hobby. Anyway, after we came back from Australia, daddy changed slightly and said afterwards that he started to look at his life and wondered where it was

29

going. We were both in our early 40's, our marriage was good, daddy and I never hardly argued as you both know, we had a good social life, sex was great and we were doing the unusual and having regular good sex, (which I learnt later on that after 20 years of marriage was rare) and we were good friends, and still are as you know.

But one day, in June the following year which was 1993, 20 years after we had got married, daddy came home from work in a bad mood. Anni you were singing in the kitchen and I was getting dinner ready when he announced that he was going for a drink as he could not stand the noise. Not something he normally did, going for a drink after work, but had occasionally started to. He had said to me that he needed to do this as the pressure he was under at work was getting to him and I accepted that, as everyone needs to unwind occasionally. It got late and he did not come home, so I rang all the hospitals to see if he had been taken there as he may have had an accident, and slept on the sofa as by 3am he was still not home. I was going frantic as we had not rowed, and I could not work it out as I thought things were OK, nothing serious going on, but the fear of the unknown was beginning to make me tremble.

All sorts of thoughts were running through my head, but one thought never ever occurred to me. In the morning he rang to say that he was coming home to collect his things as he wanted to spend a few days away and was I alright! That was the most awful shock but at least I knew he was alright and just felt numb. But the tears began. Robert you had taken the day off college as you were concerned too, and daddy came home about mid-day and went upstairs to pack but would not say anything much. I tried to get out of him what was the matter but he would not say anything. Then you tried to talk to him in the kitchen and he just ran out into the car and drove off. He had hardly said a word. You followed him in your car after pleading - really pleading with him - not to go, but you unfortunately lost him so came home and we were numb. We had no idea what was happening, or where he had gone. We stayed close together that day and evening and we were just still numb. We honestly and truly could not work out what was happening. The only thing we knew was that he was alive and not, as we had imagined, been killed in an accident.

Then daddy phoned the next morning to say that he had left us and that he was staying with Edna, a friend from hunting. You and I had NO idea. I had no idea that he was unhappy or that he was even having an affair. I had not suspected a thing. That was, in some ways, the last thing I suspected as daddy really was not the type to have an affair. We all were devastated. Words cannot begin to describe how we all felt. It was a complete and utter shock. I could not tell anyone, not any of my friends or family and for a day we just 'existed'. I could not tell anyone because I could not believe it myself. The actual words would not come out of my mouth. How could I tell anyone what had happened as I was in such shock? This was unbelievable and to me seemed unreal. He came back on the Saturday to tell me all, or tried to. He actually said that in some ways he did not know why this had happened, and neither could he explain his reasons as to why, because in some ways he still loved me and we were happy, but he wanted now to live with Edna. Wow, I was in floods of tears and thought that life could not go on. I truly could not see how I was going to get through the next hour, let alone the next day or week. We were such a close family but the bubble had burst, and god did it burst. I did not realise at the time but the ripple effect was to last for years.

But then I had to tell someone, I had to talk to someone as I was feeling that my whole world had been shattered, and I did not want to go on. So I phoned some friends, who in between my sobs began to realise what I was saying and who were just as surprised and shocked. To them we were the ideal family, they had always told daddy and me that, and in some ways envied our relationship and family life as we did everything together as I am sure you will remember. To a lot of our friends we were the perfect couple. They all said that daddy was not 'that type to have an affair' but they were absolutely wonderful. I honestly do not know what I would have done had it not been for my friends and both of you. They all came round, or phoned each and every one of them, as over the next few days, weeks and months I was inconsolable, and hysterical. I could not stop the tears and the feelings that were going on through my whole body. No one could understand or feel the pain for me. I could not eat, sleep or even cook a meal. I just existed. I was so numb, hurt, upset and felt for you both as well.

You were obviously going through such a difficult time, and different emotions to me, but one thing I do remember is you were both so upset at seeing your mum so hurt and crying so much. You both were so lovely and again wanted to take my pain away but you were now beginning to get so angry at what your dad had done. Not only to me, your mum, but to you as well. We consoled each other so much, but your friends consoled you both as well which I am so grateful for. Sometimes you could not tell me or say to me how you felt in case it hurt my feelings more, as I could not sometimes to you either. We cried together, and I tried to tell you as much as I could, and you both talked to me as much as you could but of course your pain was different. Robert to this day I can never thank you enough for the support you gave me. You were absolutely devastated and soon had to work away in Hemel Hempstead but for a long time came home EVERY NIGHT which was a 3-hour round trip to see if I was OK.

Robert, you did not want to see your dad at all and I think you had a fight most nights when you went out for six months, and broke every single bone in your right hand. Anni you went to pieces as well, but did see daddy but he would never ever discuss with you what he had done. To this day, and we are talking about over 10 years later, if only he could have talked to you I am sure you would have coped better. Actually, at the time you were only 15 but we were close and I used to talk to you about things, and you amazed me in your understanding in a very mature way. We were all-numb and could not believe that our lives had been turned upside down, and as I said none of us had had any idea that this was going to happen. We cried and cried, talked together and just supported each other as best we could. We all felt different feelings, as daddy was my husband, but he was your dad, so the feelings were different, but the tears were the same. The shock I think in some ways was the hardest feeling to bear. True shock as this was, is a deep hurting inner pain which affects every part of your body and mind. You can't breathe, eat, sleep or even think straight. Sometimes people were saying things around me and I could not even hear them. There was a time at the beginning when I had wished that daddy had died, rather than be told he was sleeping with another woman. This thought went over and over in my head so often, and I felt so guilty feeling like that, thinking those thoughts, but then at least I would have known where I was, and why he had left us all. I think that perhaps that was also one of the hardest bits, the not knowing why. I have since talked to other friends who have found themselves in the same situation and they say they felt the same. And friends that have had their partner die, they wished that they had left and gone off with someone else so now I realise that this feeling I had was normal and do not feel guilty any more.

Strangely enough, I never ever felt the need to confront his lover. You both did, but I don't think she or he ever really let you. It was as though you were expected to accept what had happened without question or explanation. Anni you did try to tell her how you felt but you could never do it face to face and there were a couple of nasty phone calls years later. You said that to tell them face to face would hurt their feelings, but I know you felt that it was partly your fault, because daddy said some very hurtful words to you which were awful and such a hurtful thing to say. I am sure he did not mean it, but of course that was not the only reason. I hope that you now realise this and have somehow forgiven him.

Daddy and I used to chat on the phone for ages nearly every day for hours sometimes, as we were both hurting, and he did come back twice. That, in some ways, was strange but he left after a short while, but each time leaving before you both came home in the evening, so it was up to me yet again to tell you that he had gone. To me that was cowardly as somehow he could not face your hurt and did not seem to think about your feelings. But on his last return home, he said something which changed my feelings about him. He went up to have a bath, came downstairs and said that he could not do this (come back) as it would upset 'her'. Well, that changed my whole thinking; as we had all

33

spent the last few months in absolute floods of tears, and were absolutely devasted and here he was saying that he could not upset 'her' after he had only known her for a few months. Excuse my language but "piss off daddy". He did not seem to have any idea of what the effect had been on us, and he did not seem to care. I am sure he did somehow but all he thought of at that time was his lover.

It is strange really but it was a few months after daddy left that I told my mum what had happened, as I really could not bring myself to tell her and just used to hide it from her as best I could. I also could not tell granddad, George, my father in law, or another relation his Auntie Florrie, as I think it was so hurtful and they would have felt let down as well. Somehow it affected the whole family, not just me and you. They were all really baffled by my actions during this time but to tell them would have made me somehow admit that all was not well at home, and I had honestly first thought that daddy would come back, which he did, but of course did not stay long. I never realised that later I would feel strong enough to ask him for our divorce.

Well, that Christmas Robert you had left college by then as you failed your exams, which you had to sit the day after daddy left, not the best timing but I am sure was not planned. You were going to travel to work in Australia for one year. I could not bear Christmas that year, so decided to go with you to Aussie to stay with my sister for two weeks, and then I went on to Brisbane to stay with some friends for a month. But, when I came back I decided that yes, I could move on, without daddy, and asked him for a divorce. It was a really frightening experience, being on my own after 20 years of marriage, with a big house to run and two teenagers to look after. How the hell was I going to manage but I had such great support from friends and a great big determination to move on, that once I had made that decision, life seemed better. I was beginning to cope on my own.

By this time, I had started going out with friends and so many of them helped me in different ways. Janet Y and her crowd started taking me to nightclubs, where I had a real eye opener and actually realised how naive I was, as I got the impression that many people at these places were married and were looking for, or having affairs. I had no idea there were so many 'single' people of my age either! I was 44. Two of my good friends who were also single, Brenda and Mandy also took me clubbing, and they together with my work colleagues were brilliant. One of them Lesley used to share driving with me to restaurants on evenings out with our work colleagues, but somehow when we drove home deep in conversation, we often got lost. How, we were never sure, but the detours we went on, we often laugh about now. The hours of talking and putting our lives to right were very interesting and somehow it always feels better after a good old chat!

Then one of my friends, but not a close friend, Janice who had left her husband a month earlier than daddy had left me, started coming out and we just gelled. The timing of our friendship could not have been better, as we were to discover. We have since been through absolutely everything together and grown extremely close. Tears and laughter, boyfriends and children and in some ways our lives have run parallel. We have always been there for each other whenever and for whatever and never judgemental. It is what I call an unconditional love and friendship. There is no other way to describe it. Janice and I propped each other up, often with the help of red wine, (too much sometimes). My very good friends Brian and Maddie came round originally just after daddy left, with a chinese meal and a bottle of port as I had not been eating or sleeping and had lost a lot of weight. They said - "Have one glass of port to help you sleep". Well, one glass leads on to two, as one didn't work for me after a while. Then I discovered red wine was much cheaper and did I drink, yes big time. I found it blocked things out and I could sleep. Many of my friends relied on a good drink too, and there was laughter and tears shed over many a bottle. I think it is a girl thing but we all had such wonderful chats and discussions and tried to put the world to rights and that is why I appreciate my friends so much.

All my friends were brilliant and I went out with them every Wednesday, Friday, Saturday and Sunday night. God, I then had to get up for work in the morning but somehow I was riding high with some sort of buzz, but it was something we all had to do. Some of the clubs we went to left a lot to be desired and were sad places when I look back, but there were others that were fun and we met some interesting people. Our favourite club was called Roberts, and Janice met most of her boyfriends there, some very interesting men I can assure you. Some of them we are not sure *why* she had to go through the experience of a relationship with them, but others were lovely and are still friends today. I have to tell you about one of the nicest chat up lines I have ever come across, and it was in Roberts. This guy came up to me and asked me if he could have one of my cigarettes, and I explained that as I smoked French cigarettes, which I did, and still do, that they were extremely strong and may make him cough and splutter. OK he said, he did not mind, and proceeded to light up. We then chatted when he told me that he had not smoked for 10 years, but it had been the only thing he could think of to pluck up the courage to talk to me - how sweet and certainly different.

We did have so much fun and laughter at some of these clubs, and I can remember Janice, Doug and myself going to two or three one night, as we could not choose one that we liked best, but we had a good laugh all evening. When they dropped me off, I was laughing so much that I tripped getting out of the car, as I was desperate to get to the toilet. I then had to climb three steps to our front door, open the door, go into the hallway and then down another step into our lounge, laughing all the way. But I tripped again, and just sat there as I had wet myself with laughter. That really was a good evening and we did have lots of them. Talking of mad evenings, one of our friends Clare will do anything for a dare, and I mean anything and if you challenge her, you never know what she will do. Dave her partner, challenged her to run around the local duck pond stark naked, after we had finished our Indian meal we were having, and of course she did. She even took off her knickers, and then sat in the back of the car on the way home still naked, and much to the amusement of onlookers! We then landed back at Janice's flat where her children were watching television with the lights out, so we thought no one was in, but Clare was still naked! I can remember my first meeting with Dave, her partner, when he carried her on his shoulders into the local pub -

what an introduction, and what a mad lovely couple they are. They both will do anything for a dare or challenge, and there is no holds barred! For Claire's revenge for the naked dash-round-the-duck-pond-episode, she challenged him to turn up naked on her front door step to take her out one evening, and of course he did, but with a bunch of balloons tied around him! I often wonder what her neighbours must have thought! Not all my friends are this mad, but we all like fun as I am sure you know.

I meet my saviour

Then, one Sunday evening in January 1994 just after my return from Australia and my decision to get a divorce, my friend Brenda and I went to one of our regular singles club, and across the room, I saw this guy and we started smiling at each other. Wow, he was something else and I honestly was not looking for romance but there was something about him. He asked me to dance and that was it. He was my saving grace as he stopped me from being bitter and twisted. He also brought out feelings in me that I had forgotten, and made me feel like a teenager again. Daft I know, but it was great, I was alive again. It is quite amazing how that feels after all those years, to be truly alive again, which is very exciting. Also, I had slept with daddy for the last 21 years and never dreamt that it would feel beautiful and natural for me to do this with someone else, but it did. It felt very right.

His name was Graham and he was ten years younger than me, and was so opposite to daddy, but I am afraid I was not strong enough and did a 'Bridget Jones thing' and I spent many an hour waiting by the phone for him to call. Why do we do it, but lots of us sadly do? He and I had a very lovely relationship, which was to last on and off for quite a few years, but he wanted children and there was no way I was going down that route. I can't tell you the number of times that when we had split up for whatever reason; I would 'bump' into him. In fact in the four years we had an on/off relationship, I bumped into him more than forty times. I lost count in the end. I can remember two particular incidents when we met on the M25. One was side-by-side in a traffic jam and going in the same direction, another was when I was facing one way and he was stuck facing the other way and I began to wonder if there was such a thing as 'coincidence'. Each time, or nearly, it prompted him to call and we would be back together. He was always late for a date which drove me mad, but he encouraged me in so many ways, especially about my work and we had some great discussions and we had a lot of things in common, and that was lovely.

But before I move on, I have to tell you about our first date. As I said, it was a mutual attraction and we had arranged to go for a drink the following week. Well, during that week, Anni, do you remember you had learnt that daddy had given your beloved horse Melody to a Riding School for the Disabled while we were in Australia, and you were so very upset as he had done this without even asking you. We both laugh about this now, but in your sort of revenge, you and a friend of yours, Louise, had gone up to London to see some friends, and unbeknown to me, had decided to make a statement. I got a call from you asking me to pick you up at the station, but I was not to be shocked when I saw you. Well, shocked was an understatement. You had got a friend to shave the whole of the back of your head of hair, and just left a few strands hanging over this big bald patch. It looked awful. Well, how was I going to explain this to Graham, who had not even met you yet? So, I made you sit on the sofa with your back to the cushions when he came in, and I told you not to get up and I would explain over a drink. Well, when I told him he just roared with laughter and loved your spirit, but understood, as he was a lecturer at a college at the time, so was used to teenagers. You got on extremely well after that.

I was beginning to learn that life can move on in a lovely different way and, as I said earlier, feeling like a teenager again was lovely and it made me realise that life is really full of surprises. I think perhaps daddy and I had taken each other for granted over the years and *we* had put *both of you* before *us*. Looking back, I think it is important in a relationship to have your own special time away from children, but we never seemed to want to do things on our own. We always included you, except when we went out in the evenings, usually with friends but, perhaps, if we had gone away on our own for weekend breaks we would have rekindled our initial romance. Perhaps we should have shared more of our hopes and dreams and talked about how we both felt more and what we both wanted out of life. But we just accepted our married life as it was because we had romance, great sex and a lovely bond but most importantly a good friendship. I hope that all of you have that in your marriages but please don't take your partners for granted. Perhaps that is where we both went wrong.

But my life was about to change, because I *had* to know that I was going to be alright and started going to 'mediums' as they gave me the reassurance that firstly Graham was my soul mate and he would be back, and, secondly, that life would move on and I would manage. One of the things that I think drew me to 'mediums' was the fact that one evening in the October of 1993, five months after daddy had left, for the very first time, daddy was going to take Edna out to a function where some of our friends were going to be and to me this was official - he was declaring his affair to the world. Well, I cannot tell you how distressed I was. I was hysterical, so I phoned one of my friends, Lesley who had also been wonderful and she came around to sit with me. Whilst Lesley and I were talking and I was crying uncontrollably, all of a sudden and completely out of the blue, I felt a strange 'tingle' go all over my body, and it happened quite a few times during the evening. I had no idea why this had happened, and Lesley then told me very calmly that there were 'spirits' in the room, and I was being looked after, and this was their way of showing me that I was not alone. It was a wonderful feeling, and a very new experience, and I was later to learn how true it was.

At this stage, I was still clubbing and drinking as I was still in a bit of an emotional mess, as it takes a very long time to get over something like this, but I had been thinking positively and was now enjoying life. Robert you and I had a wonderful relationship, as we used to talk about everything. We used to have long discussions about life! It brought us closer together in a lovely way. Anni, we were still close as well but you were going off the rails big time, stealing, lying in bed and you would not get a job, and we had enormous rows over this. You were also having tantrums about all the smallest things as well as the biggest events which were happening – it was just horrendous. The shouting and screaming, the slamming doors - all became normal, everyday events. You could not seem to speak to me or to your brother without venting some sort of frustration, and I felt you were now getting out of control. This frustration I can assure you was mutual. Your brother tried at this time to give his advice to you as he felt he was the man of the family now, but you resented it, as 'he was not your dad and should not tell you what to do". I can still see both sides of this argument and he was only trying to help me as I could not handle you, and you felt your dad did not really seem to care which devastated you. I am afraid to say that I also felt that I was not getting any support from your dad, and felt just as frustrated and very let down. It is very hard bringing up teenagers on your own

I like helping others

By this time, I had become a victim support volunteer which was something that I enjoyed and hopefully helped many people. It also gave me the idea that I would like to do counselling as a profession. So I enrolled at the local college to do a Degree in Counselling but after the first year decided that their idea of counselling and mine were different. I had been with victims that had suffered sometimes tremendous trauma and had spent sometimes hours with them, as it can take a long time for them to feel comfortable to open up, but college stated that to be a counsellor you had to give your clients one hour and at the end of the session, you had to say "goodbye see you next week". This could be just when a client wanted to tell you all and open their hearts, and I felt very uncomfortable with this. I believe that if a person who needs counselling is supported at the time of the problem, then they will not need to go to counselling years later. I know that a lot of cases are not that simple, and people cannot always get help then, and I have to say that counselling is a wonderful tool to help people move on, and very necessary for some. There are so many people who have had traumas in their lives and there is no-one there to listen, or they cannot tell anyone, so counselling helps people from all walks of life to move on. All sessions are helpful, however long or short they maybe. If only someone was there for people when they needed it, but some people feel it is very hard for them to talk about their problems, and sometimes even feel ashamed, or hurt, but if you can tell someone, even a stranger, then this helps to begin to heal the wound.

I did learn a lot about life in general during my time as a victim support volunteer and also from the counselling that I did outside of this role. Life behind closed doors is sometimes never as it seems and I hope that I was never judgemental as being a support is a far more important role.

I am scarred

Also at this time, Robert you helped me unblock a pipe in the washing machine, as there are a lot of things us women cannot do without the help of a man! But, unfortunately, the liquid that I had bought from the local DIY shop which was 98% sulphuric acid, spilt onto the floor and splashed me, causing 3rd degree burns to my neck and a little bit on my face. Bless you, you drove your car at over 100 miles per hour to get me to hospital where the staff were brilliant, but it was a very painful and traumatic experience. Especially when the consultant on a visit some months later said - "oh I know what will reduce that swelling and red scar tissue" - and then proceeded to inject 10 little cortisone injections into the scar. How I screamed. People often ask me if I have had open heart surgery, as the scar runs down my neck and chest to my breasts in a straight line. These injections did reduce the scar quite well, but the scar had pulled down my chin into my neck. So a plastic surgeon agreed to give me a mini face lift, but it all went horribly wrong. Somehow it swelled beyond belief and I had to spend six weeks hidden in doors as I had this great big bandage wrapped around my head and chin, and was covered from my eyes right down to my breasts with the biggest black and purple bruise you have ever seen. I also had a massive swelling hanging from my chin into my neck. When Janice took me to the hospital one day to have the swelling looked at, and the bandages taken off, the shocked look on her face said it all. But when the swelling went down after they drained it, it was so much better and I then had a brilliant face again.

I also went to the Red Cross who specialise in camouflage make-up and they showed me how to apply this to my neck and chest, and you can get it on the NHS. It is made in Germany by Kryolan and called Camouflage System Crème, but wonderful for any discolorations in skin abnormalities, scars, birthmarks and tattoos. I am sure if anyone needs something like this, doctors can prescribe it. Robert I remember that you brought me a beautiful bunch of flowers while I was in hospital and, this may surprise you, but no other man ever in my life has bought me a bunch of flowers other than daddy. But he only ever bought me three bunches in all the years we were married. One after each of you were born and one for our fifteenth wedding anniversary! How sad is that, so thank you.

I move into the unknown

It was now time for us all to move on. I had to sell our family home and you both certainly did not want to move. Robert, you were devastated especially but I could not afford to live there anymore. We had been there for fifteen years and it was a big step and quite traumatic going through all the family possessions, but also very therapeutic as you have to get rid of the old to bring in the new. It is hard to let go of possessions and memories sometimes, but I was moving to a much smaller house and a lot would not fit in, but I also knew that there were certain things I had to keep, but other things had to go. So I sold some pieces of furniture, which would help me buy new bits in our new house. I found a cottage in a local village and the day of the move I remember so well. It was September 1995.

It was full of fear of the unknown, I was upset at leaving our house; fearful of change but fortunately I had hired removal people who were wonderful. On arriving at the new house, the bedroom furniture had to be passed through the windows upstairs and that is not something I could have done on my own! After I stepped into our new house, and the removal men had gone, it was the most fantastic feeling, which is very hard to describe. This was 'MINE' and I could start to make my own decisions. This was a new start and a few friends since have said to me that when that happened to them, they had the same feeling which is very uplifting and positive. The cottage needed major renovations but I could see the potential, and fortunately I had a good builder friend, Bill, who I trusted, who was going to do the work.

Robert you adjusted quite quickly and Anni you settled in soon, as you met a lot of local teenagers, whom I am afraid were not all desirable, and you just 'had fun' as you used to say. No job, no money, just wanted to go out and did not care about anything else. If only your dad had told you he loved you, and you could have expressed to him how you felt. You very soon met a local guy called Anthony who was your 'first true love' but after a year you split, which was sad. Robert you at this time were still a 'Young Farmer' and had a brilliant social life with your new friends, and also with your old friends. You both had begun to enjoy our new house, but I know you still hankered after the old big house, as that was your family home, but life does not always stay the same.

I lose my mum

Something amazing and devastating was about to happen which I suppose you could call 'fate' in some ways, but I think maybe a better way to describe it is that somehow our lives are mapped out for us before we even know it!

Just after we moved into the cottage, I left my job on the local paper as the management had changed and I did not like how it was going, which was a shame as I had been there for six years and loved it and the people I worked with. So I gave in my notice. I had just moved into a cottage which needed a lot of work doing to it, but it was nearly finished. I was unemployed but decided to go to Australia for Christmas, as Robert you were going to work out there for my brother-in-law. Anni you had no job either and I had seen an advert for flights to Australia for £399 return. That was too good to be true, but this time I had no idea *why* I was going. Every other time there was a reason, but I just thought why not - cheap flight, unemployed, no ties, but what the hell. There was a reason, which I was soon to discover. We arrived just before Christmas at my sister's house in Perth, when on Christmas day we got a phone call from my two sisters at home in London to say our mum had suddenly died. She collapsed whilst spending the day with them, and died from a stroke brought on by bronchial pneumonia. I knew then the reason *why* I had come. My sister had always said that she never wanted to be on her own if anything happened to mum and dad, as she had felt very guilty going out there and leaving them as they were quite elderly by then, but of course she was not on her own, *I had been 'sent'* unbeknown to me at the time. Of course her husband and children were there too, but so was the other part of her family and it made me realise that these things are mapped out for us in some way. I had no idea my mum was going to die, or the reason for me going to Aussi on this occasion, but 'they' do. It was like it was pre-planned. Anni, you and I flew home straight away after only 5 days (a long way to go for 5 days) and Robert you stayed on to work. Maryanne then flew home for the funeral. Maryanne and I had been with my dad when he died and now my other two sisters had been with my mum when she died, so that gave me comfort.

Before my mum died, Jenny, a friend in Australia, had arranged a big 50th birthday surprise for another friend of ours, Tony C. and he had no idea I would be over. She was going to arrange for me to jump out of a big cardboard birthday cake. The look on his face would have been wonderful but of course I had to cancel this.

But, I then went to pieces. Within a short period of three years I had lost my dad, my husband and now my mum. It was too much in such a short space of time. It was like one after another, everyone other than my children and friends had gone. I think if you lose one parent and there is a big gap in the middle before the other parent dies, it gives you time to grieve properly, but not when it happens very close together. Bereavement is difficult enough to cope with, but with the loss of my marriage as well, which, in a way, you do grieve but differently, all these emotions took their toll on me. I had not had time in between each of these big events to come to terms with any of them properly. My marriage break up was difficult enough to come to terms with and I was trying so hard to be strong, but then to have this bereavement was awful.

I found that after both of my parents had died, it really did make me feel so very alone. It is a very different feeling to when just one of your parents dies, as you hopefully have had time to grieve at the loss but I found this so different. Maybe if I had had daddy or a new partner in my life at that time I may not have felt so alone, as they could have comforted me. I would have been able to share my grief and felt supported, but with all three close people to me leaving me so close together, and no partner, I really was devastated.

Fortunately at this time I was not working, as I don't think I would have got up every day to go to work, as all I wanted to do was hide and cry on my own. And cry I did, big time yet again. It is amazing how the body produces so many tears and over the last few years I had shed buckets full! Though I grieved, I had no anger or rage at injustice, as I knew that my mum was now where she wanted to be, with my dad. She missed him so much. This knowledge did really help me. A month after this happened a friends of hers had a stroke, but she was to live for a year with her brain still so active but unable to do anything for herself. I was so glad that this did not happen to mum.

I think what I also found so hard was, Robert, you were in Australia and I missed you too. Thankfully Anni you were there for me but you were still having your tantrums and screaming at me all the time, so we were still at loggerheads and this really did drain me. Emotionally and physically I felt exhausted. I know you both were grieving as well in your own way but during this time we did not seem to comfort each other. Emotionally I was a wreck and with no close partner to support me it hurt, but something amazing was starting to happen to me which kept me going.

Part Four

My fifties...tattered and frayed but saved

My eyes begin to smile

During this time, I had started meditating without my realising it. I just used to lie on the sofa and chill out or cry, it was what I called my resting time. I was hurting and although I had never been that close to my mum, it was the last straw. But, something amazing had started to happen. When I closed my eyes, I saw beautiful colours flashing before me, which was something I did not understand but accepted, as it was so peaceful, beautiful and comforting, but had no idea where they were coming from. But it started to intrigue me that yes, perhaps I was being looked after somehow. I also remembered what had happened to me on that evening all those months ago when I first felt the "tingling". I was experiencing this again as well, and it was so comforting. As you cannot create this "tingle" yourself I knew that something was happening.

I also started to hear classical music in, funnily enough, my right ear only. Now I do not particularly like classical but I would sit there and this music would start. I just let it happen because it was so peaceful. I could not explain it but it had to be coming from somewhere but this was all so new to me. Also at this time, one of my work colleagues Lesley introduced me to a friend Julie, and we just 'clicked' on our first meeting. She offered me a job helping her run natural healing exhibitions so I was starting to meet like minded people who did not laugh at me when I mentioned my "tingling and music experiences" I had to find out what I could do to learn more. So I took myself off to a book shop, as one does, and this book jumped off the shelf as I was browsing called *Opening to Channel. How to Connect with your Guide by Sanaya Roman and Duane Packer*. This book in some ways was 'sent' to me as I went straight home and could not put it down, and it opened a whole new life for me again.

I started to read this book, which helped me to 'open up' and understand some of the things which I had started to experience. The first experience I had was amazing. Yes, I had been seeing the colours and hearing the music but I was lying on my sofa with my eyes shut when suddenly a small Kodak type picture was in front of my eyes. It was as clear as any picture you might see that you pick up and in this picture were faces of people that I did not know. One in particular, and I can still see her face, was a lady from the Moll Flanders era with a white frilly bonnet on her head. She was smiling down at me and I realised that these were people 'up above' who were with me to support me. There is no other way to describe it. Over the next few weeks and months, loads of these pictures were shown to me and it is absolutely amazing. It was like having my own cinema or television screen. Then I started to see pictures on the beams in the lounge above my head. These were incredible as they sometimes moved. I was still seeing Graham on and off then, and I can remember one picture on a day when he had not turned up so I asked where he was and they showed me he was playing squash with a few friends. I asked him later where he had been and yes he had been playing squash! Wow, this was something else. I then started seeing things in the night and they would often wake me up about 4am and it was always the same, beautiful pictures as clear as clear can be. They are only small and can sometimes be feint and difficult to make out, but how it is beamed down to me, I don't think I or any of us will ever understand, as it is so wonderful. Also I was spoken to occasionally by a man's voice in my right ear, always at night, and at first I would wake up and wonder who was in my bedroom, but no, no one was there and I realised that these very clear voices were from somewhere else. If someone speaks to you, you hear it in both ears, but this was definitely in one ear only. Like the music, if it is on the radio you hear it in both ears, but one ear only received these words.

Then, in January 1997, a friend, Mandy, and I went to Egypt which was a really lovely holiday. We went on a trip down the Nile and did all the tourist bits from Luxor to Aswan, visiting the tombs and caves which are indescribable unless you have seen them. They are incredible as they are millions of years old. But what surprised me and I still laugh about it today is, on the first night of our holiday when I went to sleep, bearing in mind I was now 1,000's of miles away from home, I again started to see pictures and colours and I can remember waking up in the night feeling very surprised, saying to myself and 'them', "you've followed me, how did you know I was here". Well, of course, I laugh now as 'they' are with you wherever you go, but in those days this was all new to me, and it had previously only happened in my own home.

Unfortunately, just after we got home from Egypt my father-in-law George died which was very sad but he had suffered from his stroke for a number of years, and his quality of life was not as good as it had been. But what was nice was he was in Egypt in the war and often used to talk about how he loved it out there, and I had gone to see him just before I went to Egypt and told him I was going and he was so pleased. I promised to send him a postcard, which I did, but that was the last time I had contact with him.

Why I have put 'they' in inverted commas is because at this time I did not know much about spiritualism or any thing to do with the sub-conscious mind and all that it entails. All I knew was that we all have a soul and when we die I believe that once we, our soul and spirit, move out of our physical bodies, then this soul goes to heaven. In some ways our body is only an instrument which carries our true soul and the spirit that we know as a human person in this life time. This spirit then moves on to another realm which I used to believe was heaven, but who knows where that is.

49

But I have since come to understand that the spirit makes its transition to a different level of consciousness. From this other realm, other spirits or souls can communicate with us and it is often loved ones who have been close to us that can come through to us. My spirit guide is a spirit with greater knowledge who has evolved through many life times, and has learnt such love and compassion, that he can share and guide me. I may never have known him but he can help me by communicating through the pictures that I see or the words that he may speak to me. I also know that we are never judged only loved. It is we who judge ourselves.

I get a brilliant job

In the summer of that year, I was offered a job (self-employed) as a health care adviser with a leading health care company. Once I accepted, I was sent a learning pack. Well, you should have seen the size of it. Here I was in my 40's expected to pass all these exams. Well, I left them on the end of my sofa for about a week but I went along to the office to learning sessions, and on my first day, met a great bunch of people including Ray and a girl called Theresa. She and I walked into the building together and have been firm like-minded friends ever since. The people that I would be working with were absolutely brilliant and great fun.

A lot of people over the next six years came and went, but it was the perfect job for me. Ray and I worked together from day one, and we became good friends and respected each other and worked well together. Alan W and Colin B joined our close working partnership a few years later. But they were all lovely people to work with. We had lots of freedom if we wanted it, and there were loads of afternoons socialising down the pub. We all worked hard, and although self-employed could earn a lot if we put in the hours. There were long hours too, as nearly always there were appointments with clients in the evening, as well as during the day. A lot of my colleagues worked extremely hard, and I did also, but I had learnt earlier in my life that money was not the be-all and end-all. I saw life was a mixture of pleasure and work, and I was in a fortunate position that I did not have a mortgage to pay, which is such a relief, but others of course had to pay theirs. But, the big house is not all it is cracked up to be and it is often much later in life when we realise this. We all worked hard, but we also played hard. A group of us, and it was nearly always the same crowd, would have spontaneous social lunchtime and evenings gatherings. It was a very male orientated business, so sometimes I was the only girl amongst them and they and I had some wonderful conversations about the opposite sex, and life in general. Trust me I learnt a lot!! If an outsider could hear some of the things we used to talk about, but they gave me one of the nicest compliments that I have ever had. They said and felt that I was one of the boys. That was lovely. We had some real laughs together, but we also used to have some great days out as a Branch.

Some of us went sailing in Portsmouth, and we went go karting, and paintballing where the men took it so much more seriously than us girls. I can remember swearing at my boss Ian when he shot me in the back from close range, and, boy, does that hurt. Guys, chill-out it is only a game but the male competitiveness comes out strongly. And Andy B when he purposely crashed into my car when I was the only girl in the semi-final, well the bruise that I had on my bum was a stunner. I think one of the best outings we had was Ray arranged for us to have lunch and drinks on a friend of his boat. We went to our head office in London for our sales meeting, and then on to Edith Piaffs old boat, which was moored in St. Katherine's Dock. It was a beautiful day and the sun was shining so we all had our meal and drinks on deck, and the day flowed with laughter. They were very enjoyable. So were the sales conferences that were arranged, usually overseas and nearly always on my birthday, and we had some great laughs on them.

I think the best one was Monte Carlo. Ten of us from our office were going on this one, and I was the only girl, and I was to have a wonderful time. They were all brilliant to me and seemed to look after me, but I have to tell you what happened. When we arrived, Rod, Ray and I took ourselves off for a wander and had a drink down by the harbour, as the weather was beautiful, even though it was January. That evening, the three of us met up with the others and shared a table so we were all together, and had a brilliant evening. The next day we had to ourselves, and Ray and I hopped on a train and went to Italy for the day, where I had to buy a handbag. You can't go to Italy without buying a bag or shoes! Others went ski-ing, some to the Monte Carlo Rally or golf and we all did what we wanted. Ray and I then arranged for us all (don't forget it is nine men and me) to have a meal together in the evening. Everything was brilliant, the restaurant and company. The next day we had our sales conference, and in the evening we had a Gala Black Tie dinner.

Well, I had bought this dress from a friends shop, and I walked down in the evening with Rod, and suddenly people started staring at me. I thought nothing of it, and we had our meal and people were then telling me that they had loved my dress because they had recognised it as the style Julia Roberts had worn at the Oscars! I had no idea. It was a very simple black velvet dress, with a white stripe down the front, and a low back with a big split and netting at the bottom, edged with white. Very feminine, stylish and sexy. Earlier in the day, the boys, being boys, had decided that we should all have our photograph taken outside on the very famous casino steps, which was right next door to our hotel. So after the meal, we all gathered outside and I could not believe what happened next. The French I feel, are in some ways more fashion conscious than us British, and here I was in this Julia Roberts look-a-like dress, surrounded by nine men in their dinner suits. Well, the traffic stopped, people were pointing and staring - who was she, the expensive Porches, Lamborghini's, and such came to a halt. My shoes were hurting so I took them off, which horrified Ray but I didn't care. This was wonderful and then when we got to the steps at the Casino, again all these people were wondering who I was. They were all just standing there looking, taking photographs of me and pointing. Then this French man stepped out of his expensive car, with a girl on his arm, and came up to me, looked me up and down, took my hand which he kissed, and said

"Madame, exquisitely beautiful". Well, that was the icing on the cake for me. Then, some of us actually went into the casino, and the same thing happened. I don't think I can ever repeat that experience, as I was to be made to feel so special all weekend. Nine guys and me! I now know what it feels like to be a film star! It is so nice when you work with people who get on so well. I have been lucky with all the people I have worked with over the years, and will always stay friends with a lot of them.

I see the beauty of life

My bosses Ian and then Kym were brilliant to me, and very supportive, as Anni you had earlier found out that you were pregnant. You were 18 and two weeks prior had split with your boyfriend Simon, so you were going to be a single parent. There were still a lot of terrible rows going on at home, and I mean terrible, so you got a place in a single parent family unit with other pregnant girls, which was good because we both agreed that you could not live at home any more. The rows were too much. Then, one Friday evening I got a call from you to say the doctors were going to perform an emergency caesarean as the baby was in difficulty. I rushed to the hospital and went into the operating room with you, and the most amazing experience was about to happen. Anni you were given an epidural, covered in green sheets, and I sat up near your head, and then after a short time there was this little cry, and little Simone was handed to me. I cuddled her next to you and you were crying, as you had wanted a little girl, and then I cried as I watched as Simone's little nostrils opened and the doctor said "you have just witnessed her first breath" and then her little ears popped out and I cannot explain the experience. It was absolutely amazing and beautiful. Even now, when I recall that to friends, it brings tears to my eyes. Life is beautiful, however hard it may be sometimes.

Anni, you and Simone came back to live with me for six weeks and you both used to sleep in the same bed which was lovely to see. Simone was beautiful and Anni you were a wonderful mum, and somehow motherhood came naturally to you. But little Simone used to scream after bottle feeds so we took her to a London hospital and after tests it was discovered that she was allergic to milk and soya milk and it had burnt her stomach lining, so she had to be fed on a milk substitute. This certainly helped as poor little Simone must have been in agony. You then moved into your own flat but often came to stay and between us we looked after Simone. I was beginning also to become a surrogate mum which I was starting to enjoy.

After you had been in your flat for a while, because of your dyslexia you got into all sorts of problems with bills, and also you had no concept of money, and nearly got yourself evicted because of rent arrears when you went back to work. I helped you sort that out with the council and daddy and I tried to sort your money out but you always managed to over spend.

One morning a few years later, whilst Anni you were still in bed, Simone got up and lit a lighter in the lounge, and an armchair caught fire. She quickly had the sense, at the age of 3, to run into your bedroom, and you immediately then called the fire brigade. You were so, so lucky. The flat was ruined so you both came back to live with me. What a terrible experience fire can be and within minutes you both lost nearly everything, but you were lucky to be alive. It frightened all of us, especially Simone. Also, Anni you felt very guilty for a long time that you had not got up with Simone, but you had felt unwell again. Two weeks later you were lucky enough to be given a lovely small ground floor flat a few miles away.

I can understand why you had not got up however. You had stopped having fits at the age of ten but in your teenage years, after you started taking the pill, developed terrible migraine and often had to spend days in bed. I never realised how bad migraine can be. You used to collapse and become paralysed down one side, could not see out of one eye, could not walk straight and was very sick. Once you had been sick, then it used to subside but it could take, at your worst, four days to get over.

I learn how honesty is good

A few months later, at work I had a new boss who was into IT and he asked five of us to go with him to Derby for a week to experiment with some new technology. What a week that was. Great fun and one night four of us landed back in my room for drinks, as one does! I had got to know one of the guys over the last year, and quite fancied him, and we began a relationship. His name was Rod but we had to keep it a secret as we were working together, but to some it was obvious. Apparently our body language told it all! We did actually keep it from everyone for quite a few months. He brought out some emotions in me I never knew I had, because he is the only man I have ever wanted to pour a pint of beer over. I do regret not doing that when he made me so angry once. But it is not me, but it would have made me feel very proud of myself for truly expressing my emotions at the time. I often just let things ride over me and if I am honest, not a lot of things bother me, as I am very placid. Or if they do, I don't say anything and just go home and cry, behind closed doors, or call a friend, usually Janice, instead of confronting the issue at the time. I wish I could, but I am getting better at it and would speak up now. Even to this day, Rod and I have, and will continue to have, a lovely friendship. Over the years, Rod and I have spent many hours chatting, laughing and drinking, and often sat up till the early hours putting the world to rights. I can remember quite a few occasions, and because we worked together we were often sent on training courses and one particular time really stands out. We sat up with a few colleagues till quite late, and then Rod and I carried on drinking and talking until 6am! We then climbed into bed, got up two hours later as we had an exam the next morning at 9am, and we both passed. How we did that I am not sure, but he passed with 97%. I just scraped through on the borderline!

Another thing Rod taught me was to have honest conversations. If something was bothering either of us, we used to say "Can I have an honest conversation?" and this really is a good practice to get into the habit of. I think a lot of us don't do this, because we may be frightened of hurting the other person, but in some ways by not being honest you actually hurt that person more. I learnt that by bringing out the issues and dealing with them, they then become less of an issue. If you know where you stand in any situation, and I am not just talking about relationships, then you can deal with it. It is sometimes the 'not knowing' that can be far worse. Rod had a beautiful feminine side that he was not afraid to show to me, and taught me that men and women are so alike. We all want the same, love and to be loved, but not all of us can show it. I wish we all could. But one thing I began to realise was that I always seemed to understand other people's needs had to be put into place before mine, for some strange reason, but that he also had come into my life for a reason, and I am glad he did.

I have had quite a few other brief relationships over the years, and some have lasted a little while, whilst others I have known I do not want to see them again after just one date, but both Graham and Rod have been important to me. With both of them, I always seemed to understand their circumstances and put them before myself. I knew I had to let Graham go. He wanted to have children and I did not and I could not have lived with him knowing this. And, Rod well he had to have a relationship with his old school sweetheart and I could never be second best, but the next big romance in my life will be different. This time it will 50/50 and he will come into my life for a different reason. I know that both Graham and Rod were sent to me for a reason and I will be truly grateful to both of them for that. They both taught me different things, they both made me laugh and cry, both were brilliant lovers and both were friends who I could share and talk with for hours and hours. They both say that I taught them lessons too.

Although daddy and I split up after 21 years, I honestly never thought that would happen, and in some ways I am sorry that it did, but through the experience I have grown into possibly a different person. I feel much more fulfilled and I am now at peace with myself. A long time ago I put the past behind me, as I could not, and never wanted to, feel bitter or angry. If you both can go through life without holding resentment and if you can learn to forgive, then that would be wonderful. By being forgiving, you release the negative energy surrounding you, and in some ways if you don't forgive, you are only hurting yourself. Daddy and I are still good friends as you know, although we lead completely different lives and have different friends and interests now. The only thing I do regret is that you both in some ways are still hurting but we all now are getting on with our own lives.

The opening of my eyes

During all of this, my spiritual awareness was beginning to develop even more. When Theresa and I had started working together, we represented the company at some natural healing exhibitions and we were finding out about therapies and new age things as well as spiritualism. Some of which I must admit were a little bizarre for me. Things were still happening at home when I was doing meditations, and it was all so lovely but difficult to explain to people. I saw such beautiful pictures and colours and always had a feeling of comfort because when I was doing meditation, it felt as though someone was cuddling me and wrapping themselves around me. It also gave me a tingling sensation which when that happened, I knew that someone was there. I also felt, or was aware, that my mum and dad were with me often and because they were 'in spirit' could see and know much more about my bigger picture than I could. They could also help and guide me more now as they had a better panoramic view of all that is around me, and they actually know me better now than they ever did when they were alive. Even one of my aunt's who had recently died came through one night and said "I approve" as she now knew me much better because she had never really known me properly when she was here on this earth. Yes, we *knew* each other but didn't truly know the whole person.

I was also going to mediums still as I had to know that I would be all right. I kept asking myself HOW they knew so much about me, as I did not tell them, but then of course I knew really. I was being shown similar things myself as they had continued to talk to me in my right ear, often during the night, so it gave me confidence that everything was all going to be OK, and the comfort and experience of it was wonderful. It was beginning to make me feel much calmer about life some how and the knowledge that I was not alone was so very powerful to me. I was beginning to feel the beginning of inner peace.

Theresa and I became very close as she also was learning and experiencing similar types of pictures, feelings and often we would phone each other up, for confirmation of what we had seen and heard and what it might mean. Often these words and images became reality some time later. By bouncing off each other, we began to understand much more and we were also learning to trust that each other would pick up sometimes on something that we had not thought of, because when you are shown a picture, we have learnt that often our first gut reaction is right, but not always, as often things turn out in a completely different way to what we first thought. To give you an example, I had been shown, in the distance and quite small, which means it is far away in time, a person, but I could not see their face, lying on a hospital bed with their legs open as though they were going to have a baby. There were two doctors there, and also someone else. I had no idea at the time who this person was and of course 12 months later, Anni you had to have an emergency caesarean with me there, and I had seen this previously so I knew someone was going to have a baby, but never dreamt it would be you.

I also met a lovely lady, Cathy, who had been involved in this sort of thing all her life, and is very knowledgeable about all things to do with mediumship and astrology. Her mum is a very famous medium and she suggested that I join the development circle that she was about to start, and I jumped at the chance. Wow, I did not know this sort of thing happened to so many other people. We were to become such good firm friends, and we still are, and always will be. Here I began to trust and develop my knowledge, and had some wonderful experiences in the Circle. There is a group of us who have such a bond, and work together to give out healing, and develop our own skills, which are all different. I have right from the start had an extra strong 'link' with Cathy and a lady called Sharon. She and I worked together very closely and a couple of evenings had some special visitors who were in fact my Angels, as I was later to discover. My Guardian Angel's name is Lucy, but I also have another Angel that is often with me whose name I don't know, but I call my Special Garden Angel as she came to me first out in the open at a place called The Challis Well in Glastonbury.

This is a beautiful spiritual garden that is open to anyone. It has a natural healing well where the waters are known to have healing powers, and it is visited by people from all over the world.

Challis Well is a very special place for me, as one weekend five of the Circle members and I decided to go Glastonbury. I had never been there before and obviously had heard about the place, so was interested to find out more about it. On the first evening we visited 'The Tore' but I knew that this was not going to be the highlight of the weekend for me. I knew somehow that The Challis Well was going to be a much more significant place to me, and I was so right. After breakfast the next day, we walked to the garden. It is not a very big garden, but the feelings that you get when you are there are beautiful. Somehow this is a very magical, hidden garden, surrounded by serenity. We all drifted off to do our own 'thing'. For some of us this was to be a meditation, and for others it was just to connect our own thoughts and surroundings.

I found myself sitting on a seat by the actual well, and I closed my eyes and just sat. After a few minutes, I began to see the most amazing colours, they were all swirling in front of my closed eyes, and they were getting stronger and stronger, and the colours that I was seeing were all of nature. All the browns, greens, yellows, gold and rust, and they were like trees with the autumn shades of leaves all blowing in front of me, but all mixed into one. It was like a beautiful peacock's winged fan but in different colours. Then, I saw all the colours of the rainbow and the most beautiful blue, and then all the garden colours again, and they were just flowing in front of me. They were all surrounded by a beautiful, white light. I was surrounded by the same beautiful, white light. It was as though we were one. But also at the same time, I could feel someone wrapping their arms around me and hugging me tightly but very gently. I could not move. I just sat so very still, enjoying this beautiful feeling that was happening, and feeling this wonderful person wrapping their arms around me. It was so beautifully gentle, but strong. It was the most amazing feeling that is so very hard to describe, but it was also the most peaceful experience that I have ever had. I must have sat there for about half an hour, enjoying and embracing every beautiful moment, and then reluctantly and slowly I opened my eyes, to see Cathy standing in front of me in amazement. She had witnessed and seen my Angel standing behind me and I could not speak, the tears just ran down my face, and the words were not needed.

Cathy and I just hugged each other. There is no other way to express what we had both just witnessed. Cathy as I said has been surrounded by this sort of thing all of her life, but she had never seen or experienced anything so beautiful either and we both felt so very privileged, and special that words cannot describe it. To this day, and this happened a couple of years ago, it still brings tears to my eyes when I talk about it. I will never ever be able to describe it properly because it was such a wonderful, special occasion and I feel very special and privileged to have been chosen to receive such a wonderful loving experience.

When we were in Glastonbury, I had promised Simone that I would bring her a present back. Nothing big, but Glastonbury is not really the place to buy anything for children, but Theresa and I went into a book shop and they had some beanbag animals for sale, so I thought great, one of those will do. So, I immediately went to a little basket that had a yellow beanbag duck in it. Just right I thought, as Simone's favourite bedtime story is about a duck from her favourite book which she called the Duck Duck book. Anni you and I have read that to her so many times, so this was appropriate. Well, when I took this duck to the lady at the counter she said to me "do you want this duck, because it is a very special duck as it only has one eye". I thought about it, and decided to get another one from the shelf as this may have been cheaper, but would Simone notice? Anyway, I thought nothing more of it, packed it in my overnight bag, and after another long journey, arrived home and said to Simone, "if you would like to look in my bag you will find a little present" Well, the most amazing thing happened. She found the brown paper bag and looked inside, and then proceeded to take out the beanbag duck. Simone then said to me "nanny, why didn't you buy me that 'special duck', that was the one I wanted?" Wow, I and everyone else were speechless. We could not believe what she had just said, it was truly amazing. How did she know about the little duck over 100 miles away that I had previously picked up, just a few hours earlier?

That was an extremely powerful experience. I have since learnt that Simone and I have a very special spiritual bond that can never be broken. I am sure she will develop her own psychic abilities later in life. As a child she played for hours with her 'special friends' and always felt protected by a toy angel that I gave her for her bedroom.

My special friend

Throughout all this time, my friendship with Janice was still going strong and we were supporting each other through thick and thin. I think you both know how much we needed each other and the friendship we had was a great support to me. It is funny really, because Janice and I have had different experiences, in our own childhoods and marriages, and yet we understood each other. We experienced similar situations with our children, albeit at different times, and through this she has taught me a lot about life. As you know, she left her husband a month earlier than daddy left me, but for completely different reasons so we were both single and emotional at the same time. Our children were of similar ages and had gone to the same schools, and both our daughters are single parents, (both now with partners but not then). Our daughters both needed us more than our sons who were getting on with life in the normal way, but when your child becomes a single parent, they need your support, time and I suppose attention more.

At the beginning of our friendship, I was still living in our old house and Janice had moved to a flat quite near, and her daughter fell pregnant earlier than you did Anni, I then could not understand when she had to stay in and baby sit etc. Now I do, but her daughter needed her as she was having problems with her partner, so obviously looked to her mum for support. Also, we were both still emotional as Janice at this time had split from her new boyfriend and I was seeing Graham occasionally, so were shared a lot in common and we can both now look back and laugh at some of the things that happened, and the things that we or our partners did. An amusing example was when Janice started seeing two men, both called Mike, and one evening could not remember which Mike she had said yes to seeing so when Mike phoned to say could he come and see her she said "Yes, of course" only to find that the two men turned up together. She had a bit of explaining to do that night but she managed it! We also had the need to talk about life and this we normally did over a drink – usually red wine. I think we should have bought a wine cellar between us and had its contents delivered to our door! But it helped us along, and I must add we enjoyed lots and lots of laughs.

Janice and I are completely different characters, but one thing we do have in common is our sense of humour, and what a wonderful thing that is to have. How we have laughed over the years, about all the little and big things – it is so important to keep laughing. We both manage to find humour in even the worst times and I hope you can too. We both, at this time, were still going out clubbing, and she was getting loads of attention from boyfriends and was a wonderful flirt. Whereas I was different, and could not be bothered if I did not fancy someone enough, but Janice needed the attention. She met some lovely guys who were great for her, but there were some awful ones as well. We still laugh about some of them, but we both agree, she had to go through the experience of a relationship with some of them, why we are not quite sure! They say every one is sent to you for a reason, but sometimes it is quite hard to work out at the time what the reason is!

Because Janice in those days was not so confident, and had quite a low self-esteem, some of the things these guys would say to her were beyond me. By them saying such controlling things, she used to feel so hurt and demoralised, and did actually begin to self-harm. This is something which took me a long time to understand, and I am not sure that I ever will fully, but myself and a couple of our friends always supported her, stayed with her, helped her work her way through it, but we were never judgemental on her, I hope. It was something that she felt she needed to do, for whatever reason, and at one time she got so low when she tried to come off Prozac tablets that she had to go home to her mum for a month to get over it. We often laugh, as children never really leave you. Here was Janice in her 40's returning home to mum! I think sometimes you have to reach rock bottom, before you can begin the climb up. And she did, slowly but surely, and does not need these tablets now. She was on them for a very long time, and it took real strength and courage to live without them. These tablets, which are sometimes given out quite freely by some doctors, are I agree necessary in most cases, but they are so powerful that I do not think people always make themselves fully aware of what is in them. They are known to have side affects, and I suppose different people have different reactions, but they gave Janice the most horrendous nightmares where she used to chop herself up, had things crawling out of her, etc but she has learnt to work through these, and accept that they are just nightmares. But maybe they are related to these tablets, or her past, or a past life, not sure, but that brings up another question I often ask myself.

Why do some people go through experiences, in such a different way to others? Why do some people cope better than others? Why did Janice need to take these tablets, and I didn't. Why did Janice need to always have a man in her life, and I didn't. Why did she self-harm and I didn't? Through our friendship I began to learn that the answer has to be because we are all so different, and we are all individual people and that is what makes us the person we are. We all see and react to our own experiences as individual people. Each and every one of us is travelling our own journey, and learning our own lessons but I have learnt never to be judgemental of anyone. Nobody knows what goes on in some ones else's life and the feelings or experiences that they have. So who are we to judge? I hope you will also learn through your own lives not to be judgemental.

Another thing I have learnt from Janice's situation is that we can only be there as support. We cannot change anyone's life, only they can do it. Through Janice working through her own problems and issues, from within herself, can the healing process begin. We can guide, point out, suggest and support, but we can never own or take their pain away. This is something that someone has to do for themselves. People come to their own understandings of themselves, and their situations, in their own time. Sometimes this reality can happen to them within a short space of time. For others this can take years, and I mean years. We all can come to the stage when we can begin to start to feel at peace with ourselves. We do not all ever get there, but when we do, we can start to move on. Janice herself came to her own reality a little while ago, through seeing through her own eyes another person's struggle, whom she could relate to because she is like Janice was a few years ago. Something in Janice was awakened and we all come to our own awakening or awareness in our own time. I also came to my own awakening in my own time a little while ago.

But, by us both being non-judgemental of each other, we accept our friendship as unconditional and that is a wonderful and true friendship. Yes, we both have probably had opinions on some of the things which we have both done, or experienced, but we have both been there for each other, and tried to understand, so we have both grown from this, and I think are better people for it. We both have learnt a lot about life. I am also lucky in having other close friends with whom I have a similar relationship. How lucky I am. I hope you will be too.

I am a grandmother

Janice at this time had one grandchild whom she doted on, but when I found out earlier that I was to be a grandmother, I felt I was not old enough and I asked everyone for another name as granny or nanny seemed to conjure up someone so old and that was not me; I was only in my forties!. Why do we all assume that grandparents are elderly? This is not the case as some people in the 30's can be a grandparent. We can be young, with-it and can keep up with the younger generation at what ever age, and I certainly intended too. But perhaps my perception was because my own grandparents seemed old and out of touch, but that was another generation! But my experience of being at Simone's birth made me realise that I could not care less what I was called. Now I was beginning to understand what Janice had gone through with her grandchild, and the beautiful bond that is created.

Grandchildren are different, they are part of you, you make time for them, and you enjoy them in a different way to your own children. Over the years, I have tried to explain this to you Anni many times, but unfortunately you do not see it like that. You resented the special bond we had and because I was not around Simone '24/7'. I had more patience, and more time to enjoy her. As you know I was beginning to feel that Simone was more like my own child than a grandchild. We did so much together. I used to take her swimming every weekend, and one weekend she even had me in the pool for four hours, and we both came out very wrinkly! I used to take her to a farm she loved, where we fed the animals, or sometimes, weather permitting, I would take her to the seaside. I babysat probably once or twice a week and we had our special time together. Shopping was another favourite pastime we both enjoyed. If I knew you were both coming around to my house either just calling in for coffee or having dinner with me which you usually did, I would do all the little tasks I had to do before you arrived, or left them till later if necessary, so that I could play puzzles, play cards, but one thing that I hardly ever had to do was tell her off.

I think as grandparents you are much more relaxed and the little things really don't seem to matter, and possibly are not such a big deal as they might seem to parents. I do not mean that you are too lenient as obviously a child needs guidance, to be shown right and wrong, but grandparents I am sure are put on this earth to do a little spoiling!

When I was babysitting once Anni do you remember the time that I slept walked? I am sure you do! I had got up to get Simone a bottle, and came down stairs just as you were entering the house. You said I waved to you but I did not notice that you had company. The next morning you said to me "Mum, Richard says you have great tits!" because I had been naked. I hope never to meet him as I would be so embarrassed!

When Janice and I went shopping, it was now my turn to drag her into the children's shops and she would laugh and say – "now you know why I had to be there for my daughter" and I must say I had to agree as I loved buying things for Simone.

Janice and I were both needed, but in some ways, for different reasons as our two daughters could not have been more opposite as parents. You have been friends since school, but as parents and children, you were to put different demands on us. Janice and her daughter grew closer and she and the children even came to live with her for a long time, which did actually cause problems later. Where as Anni you and I were still struggling with each other, shouting all the time, having completely different views on how you were behaving, living your life, and how you were treating Simone, and it unfortunately turned unbelievably nasty a few years later.

I love both my children equally

Robert, you had come back from working in Australia a year earlier and I had converted part of a very large garage into an annexe which when you saw it asked if you could live in it, which was great. It had a side entrance and your friends could just pop in and out whenever they wanted, but your stipulation was for me not to put a washing machine or cooker out there, as I could still do that! When you came back from Australia you went back to the farm that you loved working on, but daddy by this time was thinking of perhaps taking early retirement and asked you if you would like to come into the firm and start to learn the business. Robert, you really did have a difficult decision to make as you loved farming, but as anyone knows, farm workers do not earn much money, and we could not afford to buy you your own farm. So you made the decision to go and work for your dad where the money would be much better. Also the long term prospects were better as well.

Now this is a difficult one. Here was daddy offering you Robert part of the business, which was to earn you quite a lot of money, but what could a transport firm offer Anni?. Should she be allowed to come and work for him and drive a lorry, or perhaps learn the paperwork side of the business, but unfortunately Anni was, and still is dyslexic, so this really was a difficult decision for us to make. Plus, this was not the sort of business that we had hoped Anni you would go into. You had good skills elsewhere and you were brilliant at sewing and had started a job looking after the elderly, which you loved and were very good at, but you also had a baby to look after so how would you have managed? A transport yard with about thirty, large lorries is not really the place for a young child. I know you could have put Simone in a nursery but you were not earning enough money to do that. But unfortunately, you did not see it like that. You felt extremely left out, hurt that Robert, in your eyes, had been given everything, and you, yet again, felt not good enough. You viewed it that Robert was again the favourite. I can't tell you how many times you threw that back in my face, and would scream how you felt at me instead of daddy.

But one thing, which I do find hard, and maybe as parents yourselves now you may come to understand and feel the same, is that I tried to treat and love you both just the same. Robert you always said I favoured Anni, and Anni you said I favoured Robert. Can't win that one, but I can honestly say I tried not to favour either one more than the other, I love you both equally. Unfortunately I have to admit that I did perhaps spend more time with Anni because of her problems at school, and I am sorry that it may have come across as favouring, but then daddy spent much more time with you Robert, but I am pleased to say that in later life, things turned around as you understood.

I learn the true meaning of unconditional love

I was still working as a health care adviser, and living in the cottage, while Anni you were living in a ground floor flat that you had been given after the fire, but you were now living with the new man who had recently come into your life, Gray. Janice's daughter and her two children had come to live with her at this time also, as her daughter was going through panic attacks. Robert you had met the girl that you wanted to marry, Elena, so life was good and we were all enjoying life, and we were all doing all the normal things in life that you do, but Anni you and I were still arguing all the time, about your way of life and some of the things you were doing.

Before Gray came into your life, you lived your life through me. I was your support, your babysitter, your close friend, but I was also the person that you took all your frustrations in life out on. For me, now and then, I am really sad and to this day I don't think Anni you realise exactly what you did, and the tears and heartache that it has caused me, and the possible consequences for Simone. This is the hardest area of my life that I am going to write about, and it has taken a long time for me to actually do this, and I am sorry if, Anni, you are going to be hurt, but it has had a big impact on my life, and I want to write about it. But also I am writing about it for you all to understand why the Angels came to me, and how they helped me get through all the hurt and kept me sane. I also at this time had enormous support from Janice, my work colleagues, you Robert and Elena and so many of my friends, who I have tried to thank, but unless someone has actually been through what I have, I wouldn't expect them to understand why I am still there for you Anni, and of course Simone. But parents do have unconditional love, and sometimes what ever is thrown at them, they can only try to help. But unfortunately, my help was thrown back at me in a way that I never ever thought a daughter would do, let alone one of my own.

Anni you were still hurting and for a long time, never really got over the split between myself and daddy, and always used to express to me how you felt, but you were beginning to try and tell daddy and Edna how it hurt, but for some reason you could just not let it go. Recently you have now made friends with them, which is so much nicer, but I have to go back a few years for you to understand how and why something awful happened recently. I could actually write another letter just on this subject as so much did happen, but it would be too painful for all the family. What is the point of bringing up the past? We have all moved on now. I wish I could say there is a happy ending, but I am afraid I can't. I do not feel the need to go into every detail of the last few years, as a lot would be repetition, but I hope that this never happens to any one of you.

Anni you have had so much anger inside you since school really, when you were bullied, had dyslexia and had epilepsy, and felt no self-worth, but trust me this anger has never been suppressed. I don't know why, but I think maybe because you hate asking for help, or admitting that you did not understand some things, but you never worked for long in any job, and just stayed in bed all day. You used to borrow money from me, and, of course, as you were not earning, never paid it back, but you were also stealing from me, big time, and from your brother and your dad. This is something that is so awful and caused so many rows, and you would always deny it, but in later years did admit it, and said it gave you some sort of buzz! I am not sure I will ever understand what you meant by that and why you did it. You would steal from my purse when I was upstairs working, and you were downstairs. You stole my credit card, and forged a lot of cheques; two of them ran into three figure sums. The total amount ran into thousands of pounds. Then when Simone was around, you continued to do it in front of her. You even told me once that you had to punish her for taking something out of a shop but how could you be so two-faced? I have since found out that you stole from some of my friends as well. Simone knew this was wrong and I can remember once when I was babysitting that Simone actually said "Mummy and Gray have been naughty when you went away" and took me to a cupboard in my kitchen, and showed me how with a pair of tweezers you had taken four packets of twenty cigarettes from a pack of two hundred, and then put the empty packets back, so they appeared to be intact. Then when I asked you for them back, (without letting you know that Simone had told me), you screamed at Simone for being a 'grass.' Poor little Simone, she understood what you had done was wrong, and I found it very difficult to witness the situation you put your daughter in, and to deal with the whole situation you had put everybody in. It was not an example of good parenting to me.

Anni you are a very good mum in a lot of ways, and you and Simone have a very loving relationship but parenting is not easy, and Anni you found it very hard to discipline Simone, without putting fear into her. It was as though you felt you had no control over your own life, and did not seem to understand that screaming over the little things, meant that obviously Simone took no notice when you screamed over the big things. I will give you one example of many, as this one Anni you and I have discussed many times, and you just laugh, but I think it explains very well how hard it was for me to stand back and not interfere, which I am afraid I did.

I remember Simone being about three and she had long hair which you had put into bunches. Simone was playing on the floor with a puzzle, and you said to Simone "Come here Simone", and because Simone did not immediately jump and run, you started threatening her with "I'll tell you one more time, come here. If not, I will count to five and if you are not here then, then you will be punished". You repeated this over and over again. Of course, Simone by this time was quivering and was frightened to go to you as she thought obviously she was going to be told off, but had no idea what for, as all she was doing was a puzzle. Then Anni you started counting "five, four, three Simone, come here, two, one". By this time, Simone had run onto my lap, which infuriated you, and then screamed "Simone come here". When Simone did actually go to you, do you know what you did? You said to Simone "I just want to adjust your bunches as they are coming loose". Well, how can a child know the difference between having her bunches

70

adjusted and running across the road, without looking, when your mum screams at you for both? But it was very hard for me to watch Simone and your battles with each other. Simone loves you to pieces as her mum, and when Anni you are in a good mood, you are a lovely mum and will spend hours playing with her and taking her to places. But if things are not going right, then you used to take it out on either me, or Simone. This I find very unfair, and it is difficult to stand back and say nothing. Simone is only a child and you sometimes set her the wrong examples.

Also, the way you used to talk to me, horrified me and some of my friends who were unfortunate enough to witness this on quite a few occasions. I am a very placid easy going person and most people who know me would never think that I would argue, let alone raise my voice. Why and how I put up with it for so long is a mystery to me now. You would never ever have dreamt of talking to daddy like that so why did you do it to me? I have to ask myself why did I let you. I am normally a very strong person but it somehow just became a way of life and it had got out of control. I somehow could not deal with everything emotionally because over the last few years so much had happened and I did not have the extra energy I needed to continue to cope with you. Everything was so draining and exhausting but I was trying to be strong for my own sanity.

If, Anni, you were in difficulty, I would be the first person that you turned to, and you did on numerous occasions, and I always helped. I had always in some ways protected you right from an early age, maybe this was wrong. You found reading official letters hard, and sometimes it was easier for you to hide their contents than face them. When you first moved from the mother and baby unit into your flat, you were threatened with eviction because you had gone back to work, and come off benefits, but the hours that were available to you to work, were not enough for you to earn enough to pay all your bills, and through a misunderstanding, the rent was not paid, so hence an Eviction Notice was sent to you. I helped you sort it out, and thought nothing of it. (A parent is there to support a child, regardless of what happens, and this is what we call unconditional love). I also helped you with your bills and bought you food when you had no money.

Another incident happened recently when I was prepared to help, but was reluctant to just hand money over to you to solve the problem. It was what you expected though, that I would always bail you out, but this time I said no. I had done it far too often, (and you were still not paying me back), but there was a warrant out for your arrest. Rather than sort it out, you were just going to hand over the money to clear your name, and you wanted me to give you more than £400 - excuse me, no not this time. I knew that the fines that you were being chased for were not all yours, as the car in question had been stolen and burnt out and it was quite a simple thing to sort out. So I did - I explained to the police, and the insurance company, and wrote down all the relevant details for you to hand to the magistrate next morning. The police had agreed that if I took you to the police station in the morning, they would have to arrest you and put you in a cell for a few hours but they would let you go before a magistrate to explain what had happened. You had actually been to see a solicitor but he was not available, so I collected you and Simone in the morning, looked after Simone while you went to court, who listened to the evidence and reduced your fine to £90 which you could pay off at £5 per week. Brilliant news, and you did actually thank me, but later this was thrown back at me and I was accused of f.....g interfering. Of course, you now had Gray to support you, so it was not long before I was told "I would not be needed" anymore.

Simone had found it very hard when Gray suddenly moved into your flat, so soon after the fire, as she hardly knew him but she liked Gray which was good. However, for four years the major people in her life had been just me, her nanny, and you her mum, and we all were extremely close and you both would do everything together, including sleeping in the same bed which I think is lovely, as it does create a lovely close bond. But now Gray was to share her mum's bed, and she was expected right from the start to sleep in her own room. You both did do the bedroom up for her in the colours that she wanted, but, of course, it was strange for her, and she found it very hard to sleep all night all on her own just like that. If it could have been a gradual process then I think things would have run a lot smoother, but I am afraid that it caused major arguments with Simone being disciplined and shut in her room for long periods of time. To me, I think that would make the matter worse as this was the room that she did not like sleeping in, and should have been made a special place, but I think she thought of it as her punishment room. When ever I baby sat for Simone, she would sleep in my bed as she had done right from a baby, and as she did with you, her mum, and there is nothing nicer than in the middle of the night when I had perhaps gone downstairs to get her a bottle when she woke up, and for her to snuggle up to me when I put my arm out, and she would say 'I love you nanny' and then we would curl up and sleep. That really was very special.

I loved having Simone either during the day or evening, usually once or sometimes twice a week, and it was our special time. That's what grandparents are for. We do have a special bond, and Simone's and my relationship was no different to other grandparents. Or maybe it was slightly different as you both had lived with me for quite a long time, and you both used to spend a lot of time at my house, popping in nearly every day, so in a way she was more like my own child than a grandchild. But this happens in so many households, where children are often brought up between parents and grandparents, and especially perhaps with a single parent, as they do need help. Simone was also attending the local children's nursery in the village that I lived in, and they loved her there. Simone is a very sociable child, and loves adults as well as children and they used to say what a smashing child she was, as if they told her off, she just shrugged her shoulders and said 'OK' and moved on to something else. Quite unusual for a child, and she never got stroppy or sulked as some children do. But this was the same for me, whenever I had to discipline her for something, which I must say was not often, she just accepted it, and I never ever had to shout at her. But of course, this was the opposite to what was happening at home with you.

73

Simone, in some ways, was very mature for a child, and was learning also what was right from wrong, and was noticing how different her mum was to the rest of the family. Neither daddy, Robert nor I used to swear but I am afraid that Anni you swear all the time. When she was a little older, you and Gray said that it was OK for her to swear in her own home, as this was becoming the norm as far as Simone was concerned as you both swore all the time. But I didn't and still don't, (well maybe occasionally), but one day, Simone and I were in the kitchen, and she dropped something and she said a swear word. I did not say anything, and just turned around to look at her as she suddenly burst into tears and said 'sorry nanny, it just slipped out'. Here was this little child, no older than four, knowing that to swear was wrong, and I just cuddled her. There were no words to say.

Before Gray came into your lives, Anni, you unfortunately were not a very good housekeeper, as you never cleaned your flat and you normally used to cook just junk food for you and Simone, but occasionally, if you could be bothered, you would cook. Now Gray does all of this, and I must say he is a good cook. He does all the cooking, and house work so I am not sure actually what, Anni, you did with your time. You did not work for a long time. Gray thinks the world of Simone, and Simone loves him, which is nice, and he has been good to her in some ways, but Gray has had a very sad upbringing and was brought up for a period of time in a children's home, and he has had a spell in prison, so the closeness of a family may not have been available to him, and now Simone was not being allowed to be cuddled, as you both now considered this to be molly coddling. Oh, how can a child of five not be allowed cuddles? I still find this hard as both of you used to love to curl up in bed with us sometimes in the mornings, or sit and cuddle on the sofa, and both you Anni and your brother did this up to when you both left home, which was in your teenage years, or older so I could not understand why you thought like that. I am afraid that I have to say that I think this has to be Gray's influence as Anni you have always been a very affectionate person, to your family and your friends. So this was another area that you and I differed. I continued to cuddle Simone, if she woke up in the middle of the night in her own room (as I was following your wishes) I let her creep into my bed for a cuddle, as she had always done, but oh no, according to you this was not allowed!

Simone was also not allowed to wear any feminine clothes and pink was banned from her wardrobe. It was as if you were trying to bring her up as a boy. Because Gray did not like pink did not mean that other feminine colours could not be worn. She is a girl after all and she liked to be and do girly things.

Anni your behaviour was of grave concern to your dad and me, as you well know, and it separated you from your dad for quite a long time, and certainly did not help matters. You just used to swan about from place to place, drop into see friends and only stay for a short while, you hardly ever went to work, so Simone was not having a stable life, and certainly had little or no routine, until Gray came into your lives. Then it went to the extreme in my view, now Simone was being over disciplined. She was also being threatened continually that if she misbehaved, Gray would leave. She started school just before she was five, but up until then, Anni you, and therefore Simone, found it hard to fall into a routine of any kind. Actually, I took her myself to her first day of school, as you felt you might have got upset leaving her, and she fortunately loved school.

Often Simone would express her thoughts, as she was growing up and developing her own character, and what a lovely bundle of fun she was growing into as she was always laughing and never nasty. If she could, she liked nothing better than to make someone laugh, and she learnt this from quite an early age. We both had our little jokes that we shared, but I am afraid that Anni you were beginning to discipline her through fear. It seemed the only way that you could control her - and the screaming that went on was awful to listen to. And I mean awful. You just used to swear at Simone, shout and really scream at her. We have spoken about this often and I found it so hard to stand back and say nothing. Especially when some of the things that Simone was shouted at for were for such little things, of which I did give you one example earlier - about the bunches, but I could list others as this went on for years, but what is the point? This behaviour towards little Simone was the norm.

But, she is a strong character and could stand up for herself, but of course she was then punished, where as Anni you could see that I did not need to shout and scream at her, and Simone was always coming to me, rather than to you, her mum, and I can tell you this really annoyed you. Why were you so jealous of the bond that I had with Simone? Rather than take stock of how you dealt with things and perhaps look at the reasons why Simone always came to me, you just never seemed to want to change how you handled things. Simone did misbehave with you, I agree but you seemed to be far more interested in telling me about all the things you had bought for her to go in her bedroom, as if buying material things was more important, and by doing this, this was your way of showing her you loved her. She knew you loved her so I cannot understand the need to do that.

I am afraid that social services were called in, because one of your friends phoned them, with accusations of bruising (that were proved to be unfounded). I have to say that I am afraid a lot of your friends were also concerned with the way you were behaving. But even Anni you admitted to them that you found it hard to discipline Simone, and you did actually agree to go to a parenting class, but after one session, decided that Simone was your child and no one was going to tell you how to bring her up! (Actually I have been polite in what you said.) But what you were also doing was listening to some of your friends about all the 'rights' that you all seemed to think you had, and some of them were very influential in your thoughts. Why has your generation suddenly decided that you have these 'rights?' Every family's circumstance are different and what is right for one family may not be right for another, but you did not take this into account. As far as you were concerned, if you didn't like something I had done then, instead of addressing the issue with me, you thought nothing of taking the matter further outside of the family as some of your friends had done.

I cry so much

But then the situation became much worse. Simone wanted to come and live with me, her nanny. The rows that were going on at home had become too much, and Simone had said so many times over her very short years that she would rather live with me. Sometimes Anni you would have to drag her home as she was screaming and crying that she did not want to go home, that she wanted to stay with me, and one awful day, things got really bad.

The night before this happened, I had been at a Circle meeting and we had done a Tarot workshop and one of the members, Anthony, had tried to do a reading for me, but he couldn't, as he felt so very sick at what he saw in the cards. Well, Anthony can be a little dramatic so I did not really take any notice, until I got a phone call from you early in the morning the next day. I immediately phoned Cathy as I began to shake, and she calmed me down and suggested I took control, as little Simone (at the age of 5) had packed her own bags. You were screaming that "the little shit wants to come and live with you, her nanny", and that you were "bringing her over and I could have her, as far as you were concerned". God, what an awful day that was. I was shaking, I felt sick and wondered what on earth had gone on, but when you both turned up I was in for an even bigger shock.

Simone was absolutely white, and carrying some of her belongings. She was crying, shaking, but so very, very quiet. She had obviously been through a lot at home, and was now very frightened, and just ran into my arms for a cuddle. She sat on my lap, hanging her arms around my neck, was still shaking, crying and was as white as a sheet. But I think one of the things that struck me so quickly was how quiet she was. I felt sick. And you, her mum, were screaming, screaming like I have never heard before. "If you little shit want to come and live with nanny, then you will never see me again, as I will disappear as I don't want anything more to do with you". God, little Simone could say nothing, but held on to me like she had never held me before. She was still shaking, could hardly speak, and just kept saying that she wanted to live with nanny. I suppose in a way she has always felt I am her second mum and she has always felt safe with me. Of course, this angered you more, so the screaming went on, and on and on until I could take it no more.

Somehow, and to this day I am not sure how, I managed to calm Simone down, and just sat and cuddled her. But, what I also tried to do was to ask you how you would really feel if you went away, and never saw her again. And over and over again, you said that you didn't care, but of course I was sure you did. I tried to say to both of you how lost you both would be without each other, but I also had to say to Simone that she could not come and live with me as that would be wrong. How that hurt me, but to this day, I do not think that it would have been best, as she would have missed her mum so much, and you would have missed her too. But, it took quite a few hours of gentle persuasion for Simone to go home to your house, and for you to calm down. I felt so awful, for a long time afterwards, telling Simone that she could not come to live with me, because she had really wanted to. After you both left, I just sat and cried. I cried for a long time, as Simone had been in such distress, and it hurt me. To see a child, let alone your grandchild, in such a state, is an awful experience, and it was Simone that I felt for. She is just a child.

But this was only the start - more hurt and tears were about to happen to break my heart. It is strange really as one evening in Circle a few weeks earlier; Cathy had told me that the 'Sister of Mercy', a very special Angel, would be with me. Well, she normally comes when there is going to be a death, or grief in some way, and when she told me this, I had no idea then why this Angel would be coming. I was about to find out a few weeks later.

Also at this time in our lives, your brother and daddy had both come to the decision that they really did not want anything to do with you, and, of course, this hurt you, but you still did not seem to realise why. In your eyes, they could go to hell as far as you were concerned, but you did try to see them, but it did get to a stage a little later where Robert made the decision that life was far more pleasant without the aggravation that went with his sister. To this day he still does not have anything to do with you, and has not spoken to you for over two years. He made this decision because he wanted to put his family first, and Anni you did create some really awful situations and scenes. Daddy and Edna had distanced themselves from you, and did not speak to you for a very long time. That actually made *me* very cross because I needed his support, (which I am afraid I felt that he did not always give me,) as I felt so alone in dealing with all the aggravation from you. But for him it was easier to walk away I suppose, and I have to agree that it was a continuous battle, and is very draining. We all felt emotionally drained, and I am sure that Anni you must have felt so too, but you did not let up. Your anger just boiled even more.

I am put to the test

At work, I was getting sometimes up to six phone calls a day from you and my work colleagues Ray, Colin and Alan just knew from my face when the phone rang who was at the other end. Colin was especially good as he understood what was happening, as his wife had experienced something similar with one of her children, so he knew the heartache that was going on. Ray and Alan were very supportive, and I think just felt for me - they couldn't do anything else. But also at this time, I was working on a new laptop presentation with the health care company for a new product that they were about to launch, and I was one of the people who was asked to represent the company on a customer marketing weekend. This same weekend I was about to experience another cancer scare. After the shock of daddy leaving, it had brought about the start of my change. (And how brilliant that is, because you don't have to suffer the monthly period anymore and this is great.) But, in the middle of a presentation, I started to bleed. Hell, what was happening, as this had not happened for over two years, so, of course, I was a bit concerned. I had spent the previous night chatting to all my colleagues but in the morning, after I discovered this 'blip' I suppose my mood changed and I became very quiet but could not tell them what had happened, as the weekend was not over.

But one of them said to me what a strange person I was, as one minute I was so full of life and chatty, and the next minute I was so distant.

Oh, if only they knew. So I went to my doctors on the following Monday morning, who immediately proceeded to tell me that "The NHS has made a commitment to see cancer patients within two weeks". Well, this concerned me even more and two weeks can seem like a very long time - I really did not need this. With all that was going on at home, but I decided I would just deal with it. Somehow, I would get through and I was not going to let it get me down, I had done it before, so I could do it again. So, through the company that I worked for, I went to see a private consultant the next day. Janice came with me as I really was not prepared to go through this alone, and I was given some tests, and I was advised that they would like to operate straight away, and investigate as they were not sure what was going on either. So, although this was happening very quickly, I was prepared for the worst, and Janice drove me to the hospital where I had some investigations done. But, I also had to wait a week for the results, which fortunately came back negative of cancer, and to this day the specialists really do not know what happened. I am sure the stress of what was happening at home had a lot to do with it. Stress shows itself in lots of different ways.

But this customer marketing weekend turned into another career for me within the company. I still had to work as a health care adviser, but I was asked to help test a new product that they were launching on laptops, and then once I had learnt all the in's and out's of it, I was to be part of a team that would train my colleagues, and I surprised myself by loving it. I had found a new vocation. I really did enjoy the teaching and was very nervous on the first day, and then it just sort of flowed. But what a scary thing it is to stand up and teach, never having done it before, especially to people that you know. So the Sunday before I was going down to the head office, I decided to take my old boyfriend Graham's advise and to firstly check that I had everything, secondly, to know exactly what I was talking about, and thirdly, if I didn't then to say so.

This was the best advise that I could have had, because I cancelled my friend Theresa coming over for the day, and I went through everything, so I felt confident when the time actually came. It is far better to say honestly that you don't know something, than try and bluff your way through. Graham used to stand up in front of hundreds of people and give lectures and that piece of advice I found invaluable. But, I had learnt as much as I could, so when the time actually came for me to do my presentations I was fine. Actually, I thoroughly enjoyed it and Jules, one of the trainers and I made a good team. What I found so interesting is that you can have a class of 8-10 people and some people pick up instantly what you are conveying to them, but others you can show them time and time again, and they find it hard, but funnily enough it was not always the youngsters that were the most computer literate. Oh, how some of my colleagues hated it, and actually some still do, as when you have been a sales person all your life, and maybe in your 40's or 50's, computers can be very frightening, and technology does not always come easy.

I also enrolled on a course at a Life Coaching Foundation which I could do part-time as this is something I find so inspirational and wanted to train to be a Life Coach. I still am learning so much about life, and I enjoy every aspect and will pursue this career at my leisure.

I see friends and family move on

Janice at this time was again being very supportive, which I am so grateful for, and we had many social evenings out together. We still found comfort in red wine, and had many a laugh over a bottle or two. Janice's daughter and her two grandchildren had come to live with her, which was to turn out to be quite a strain. But, she was beginning to get very depressed with the situation and was thinking of embarking on a completely new adventure, which was to materialise a year later.

A lot of my other friends were also moving on with their lives and moving all over the world. I do miss them, but still see them but not as often as I used to. I have learnt that life does move on when we are ready and we each have to do what is best for us. A lot of my friends have now got new partners and this has taken them on to the next stage of their own lives but whenever we meet the fun and laughter is still the same. But somehow it is not the same as when we all used to see each other regularly. Fortunately some of them and my Circle friends are nearby and we do socialise a lot which is brilliant, and the friends that have moved abroad? Well, I thank them in some ways, as I can now have cheap holidays! The friends that have moved to other parts of this country, I thank also, as I can have nice weekend breaks. The socialising will still continue wherever we are, and the girl's nights and dinner parties that I and other friends organise will also continue, as when they all come home, it is a good excuse for a party and you both know that I like nothing better than that.

Robert you were working for your dad now, and had started right at the bottom of the company driving one of the vans, which you actually quite enjoyed. Daddy wanted to retire so you were brought into the office, where you have to be on call 24 hours, week on/week off, but it was a good move in some ways, but you found office work different. You loved the outdoors, and even driving had been outdoors, so it was a new experience, which took time to adjust to, but you were up for the challenge. But, you had also fallen madly in love. You had quite a few girlfriends and were not short of admirers, but once you had gone out with them, then, to you, the challenge was over. But Elena was different.

A few years earlier, you had gone up to stay with one of your college friends James in Cambridge and you both had gone to a nightclub, where you met Elena and your relationship was to begin. Elena was different to your previous girlfriends, and would stand up to you and challenge you. So after a courtship of about a year, you both decided to get married and to buy a house together. I can remember the day Robert you proposed to Elena, which was full of tears and joy, and I had said to you that I was going to leave my old engagement ring to you in my will, but if you ever wanted to use it for your own engagement then you were very welcome. Much nicer than sitting in a safe for a long time, as it was a lovely three stone ring, and I was not going to use it again. Elena had lived in Bedford so it was easier for her to move down here and get a job in London, as of course Robert you needed to be near the firm, so you bought a little house about ten minutes drive from me, and lived there for a couple of years. Just after you both moved in you went on a holiday to South Africa on a safari, and upon your return Elena became pregnant. It never quite works out how you plan things sometimes!

Daddy and I liked Elena very much, but it is also very strange when your son meets someone and you have to get to know each other. Very different from a daughter and her boyfriends. I really did not have any doubts about Elena making you happy and as far as I was concerned, then I was very happy for you and I hope never tried to get in the way. Robert you and I had a very close relationship and I think that for a while, Elena was a little wary of the bond that we had, and there were a few up's and down's to start with, but now Elena knows that I am not the interfering mother-in-law type, we have a lovely relationship, but there was also a time when Anni and Elena were quite close, but through various misunderstandings, they are not friends now, which I feel is a shame, but understandable.

A few years ago when Robert, you and Elena had bought your first house, I can remember cracking up with laughter one day as you paid me a lovely compliment when you said "mum I think you should grow up and stop acting like a teenager" and you couldn't understand how flattered I was because you were now the serious one with a mortgage and family - which is called responsibility. Whereas now, I am on my own, footloose and fancy free and I can do as I please and can go out as and when I want!

As I said, Elena had fallen pregnant after the holiday, so the wedding plans were put on hold, but this time her pregnancy for me was so different to Anni as, of course, I am Anni's mother, and therefore much more involved with her. With Elena, she had you Robert, which of course is how it should be and therefore, Robert, you were with her when she went into labour in May, and six hours later, little James was born. I was about to become a grandparent again. I went to see this little bundle of joy with beautiful strawberry coloured hair, only to find Elena sitting up, tanned and fully made up, and looking as though she hadn't been through anything. She looked great, and here was my son holding his own little son. What a lovely moment that was. You were so proud and so was I. But I was naturally to have a different relationship with James to Simone, because with Simone I had been there at her birth, and also she came to live with me for a long time. But, of course Robert, you and Elena had a good, healthy relationship and both managed parenthood very well, right from the start. Also, if Elena needed someone, she would turn to her own mum, but I was beginning to feel a little guilty, because I was so wrapped up with what was going on with Anni and Simone, that I did not see as much of James as I should have done, or would have liked. Of course, I did do some babysitting, but not as much as I did with Simone and I felt sad about this, but on the other hand Elena has brilliant parents who love to have James and do have him all the time. Actually her dad did say to me that because he was away in the army for much of Elena's childhood, he was not going to make the same mistake again with James, so is making up for lost time, and loving every minute of it.

So little James was here, and you then decided to get married. You both had previously wanted to get married abroad, just the two of you, with a few family and friends, but things were different now you had James. You both looked at all the local venues but things seemed so expensive, so a venue back near Elena's parent's home in Bedford was chosen. Robert you did have a few doubts about the wedding, because of the cost, and you felt that why would a piece of paper make you any happier than you already were. You also somehow wanted reassurance from me that you're marriage would not turn out the same as your mum and dad's had done. This really took me by surprise, as your wedding was such a long time after my divorce, but it was still in the back of your mind, and oh, how I felt for you. But, I could not give you a 100% guarantee that your marriage would last forever and ever, as I had honestly thought mine would. I think most of us do at the time of our own weddings, but no one knows what is around the corner, or how things will turn out, but you both wanted to be together. You work well as a couple; you both love your son to bits, and are a normal, happy family. Elena had never gone through a divorce with her parents, so could not fully understand how you were feeling, but was very patient, and tried to understand. So, Robert you came to your own conclusion that you wanted to spend the rest of your life with Elena, and James and that marriage does bring with it 'completeness' within a relationship, which is difficult to define.

So, all the arrangements were made, and you both decided not to have a great, big wedding, but a close wedding with the people that you wanted to be there, and who were part of your lives. But, you both decided Anni was not going to be invited. She was not a part of your life anymore, and daddy and I tried to persuade you that she was family, but you were frightened right up until the actual time that you said "I do" that she would turn up and create a scene, and that is the last thing you want at your own wedding. How awful that must have felt for you, and also Elena. I never realised that until you told me later. So, my invitation was to Simone and myself only.

I go to the wedding on my own

Now this one was going to be difficult for me, as at this time I did not have a partner, and daddy had, in the previous year, got married to Edna. I did feel extremely awkward, as I felt that somehow I was letting you, my son, down and also myself. I had not been in a serious relationship since Rod, but Rod and I were still very good friends so he agreed to come to the wedding with me, and I was so pleased. I know this may seem silly, but it was important to me to have a man by my side, but not just anyone. I know Janice's sister had felt the same when her daughter got married, because if you are on your own, it is very hard to watch your child get married, when their dad is with someone else. I suppose it is because when you have children, it is the parents' dream that they will meet someone who will make them happy, and you automatically expect to be at their wedding together. Not

85

that I had any misgivings about daddy and Edna being together and getting married, that is not what I am saying, but it is a time when it does make you feel very alone. You are an important part of the ceremony, and you want your children to be proud of you, but I felt that I was letting you down somehow. Yes, I had had quite a few men in my life since my divorce, but no one that I wanted to settle down with, and spend the rest of my life with, as I had not been lucky enough to meet him yet.

Janice understood how I was feeling, as her sister had been through the same experience, so she knew how important my outfit was going to be, so off we went to the shops together. She had always been with me when I went ball gown hunting for the company sales conferences, and I knew that I could rely on her judgement. But, over the years I had put on quite a lot of weight, and was now a size 14 or 16 but that was not my problem, my problem was my stomach. It seems so out of proportion to the rest of my body and I am very conscious of it sticking out, and the only way I can describe it is, it is like a man with a beer gut, but I am a lady! Mine is a wine gut. So, outfit after outfit I tried on and one or two were OK, but they did not make me feel special, and I wanted to feel special as this was the day my son was going to get married. Also I wanted to wear a hat. I am not a hat person, but occasions like weddings I think need a hat to complete an outfit. So I had previously phoned daddy to ask if Edna would wear a hat, and she loves them, so no problem there. My sisters also agreed to wear a hat, as did Janice and another friend who came, Mandy, but Elena's mum decided not to, so should I, or not? Yes, I wanted to wear one but decided to see what outfit I felt comfortable in first, and if it called for one, then one I would wear. I then found a red dress and jacket that Janice and the shop assistants said looked stunning, hid my stomach much better than other outfits had, and was extremely classy, as I have always dressed well, and love to look good. But, the outfit was finished off with a big red hat and handbag to match, so what the hell. I liked it, and so did everyone else and it made me feel good about myself. Actually, at the wedding my sister Liz was amazed when she saw me, and said how lovely I looked, and Elaine the photographer said I looked stunning; as did five other people who were there, including one of the receptionists who did not even know me, so I was so pleased. Robert you laughed at your mum in a hat, as I don't think you had ever seen me in one before.

The wedding was a beautiful occasion, and was made extra special I think because we had booked rooms for us to stay over, as did a lot of your friends, so it made it much more relaxed. Rod unfortunately could not make it at the last minute so my friend Mandy came in his place. When we arrived, we all had coffee, went up to our rooms to change, and then I made a big mistake.

Anni, you had not let Simone come to the wedding, as you yourself had not been invited, so why should you allow your daughter to go. Simone was very disappointed as children love weddings but as it so happened Simone got chicken pox, but her spots had nearly cleared so she could have come, but no. So, when I was in my room changing with Janice and Mandy, I did what I would normally do everyday and phoned to see if you were both OK. God, I got screamed at. "How do you think I feel on the day my brother is getting married and I am not allowed to be there"? Now, if I had not phoned, I would have been wrong as you would have said I was too busy to care about you, so either way I could not win. I thought I had done the right thing, but it was to have a major consequence a few days later, when my nightmare was about to happen.

I am in deep shock

We all had a really lovely time at the wedding, and you both looked wonderful and happy. After a leisurely breakfast the next day, we all made our way home. Robert you and Elena were going off to Canada snow boarding, and you had bought the mothers, a beautiful dried flower arrangement, which of course I took home. On the Monday, which was 17th February, 2003, Anni you and Simone came over after school, as Simone was eager to hear all about the wedding. Anni you quizzed me on the flowers, and got quite stroppy and we landed up having a very big argument, you screaming at me and me screaming at you. Well, I did not often scream at you, that was normally something you did, and Simone got a bit upset as she had never heard her nan scream at her mum, and this was unusual. It's funny really because she was so used to you screaming at me, that she took no notice of this, this was normal to her, but as I said she did get upset whilst she was sitting on my lap. But, Anni you stormed out after a little while, along with Simone of course, and the next I heard from you was the biggest shock of my life.

You had gone to a solicitor to stop me seeing Simone. You took the greatest of pleasure in telling me, over the phone, that I was never, ever, ever going to be allowed to see Simone again, and I was to stay away from you both, and also I was not needed any more. I was also to expect a solicitor's letter in the next few days, which was to tell me of my rights, and did I know that grandparents have no rights, so tough, and that I was not to get in touch with you either. But, if I wanted to fight to see Simone, then I would have to do it thought the Courts, as you were taking me to Court. God, I cannot describe how I felt. My whole world seemed to crash in on me, and I truly could not believe what I had just been told. You had meant every word that you had said, but what was even worse, was the pleasure that it seemed to give you. Do you know, you actually laughed as you put the phone down?

To this day, I can't actually remember what I did over the next few days, until I received the solicitor's letter, as I was in shock. Shock, that you my daughter would do something like this to me. I again trembled inside, and I could not stop shaking and crying as my mind could not take in the horror. I know that, of course, Janice was the first person that I told, and she could not believe it either, and she just came round and cried with me, as she knew everything that had happened. I also phoned Ray at work and told him because I had to cancel all my appointments, or get him or Colin to go on them for me, which they did - bless them - as I could not go to clients crying. I remember I phoned Cathy and both Theresa's as they are also close to me, and knew of the struggles that I had been having, but I could not speak to them properly as I was just numb and crying all the time, so in-between sobs, I told them what had happened. They were speechless, as was everyone else later when they knew. But until I actually had the solicitor's letter in my hand, I was trying to think that this had been a bad dream, and that it would all be sorted out, and you would either change your mind, or I had been mistaken in what you had said.

But no, I was not mistaken. The solicitor's letter arrived about a week later, and what a hell of a week that was, and what a hell of a time I was about to have. The contents of this letter I still, to this day, find hard to believe and it was to cause so much grief, with not only me, but within the whole family as obviously I had told daddy and Robert what you had done. They were both horrified and shocked as I had done so much for you and been your support for so long.

In this letter I was accused of only three things. One, I was not respecting yours and Gray's disciplinary rules as the parents. Two, that I had given Simone Coca-Cola when you had given me instruction not to let her have it, as you said it made her hyperactive, but also that three, I had let Simone sleep in my bed when she stayed at my house, and again that was not allowed. That was all I was accused of. I was also to attend mediation, and "pending a mediation appointment", I was asked to "refrain from contacting their client." So it was true, I could not see Simone. And oh, how daughter you loved every minute of it, as I was about to find out.

I cannot believe what is happening

Of course, I wrote back to the solicitors straight away, agreeing to go to mediation, but also with a letter expressing my deep concern as to the damage this was going to do to Simone, and also the hurt that this had caused, which seemed to be of no concern to either of you. Before the appointment was sent through, Anni, you and I had spoken a lot on the phone but to no avail and you were just determined to go through with this, regardless of the consequences. Simone and I were hurting, and I was hurting like I have never hurt before. This was different, as a child, my granddaughter was involved, and on several occasions you had been at Janice's house when you and I spoke, and I could hear Simone screaming in the background that she wanted to see her nanny, and she was crying hysterically. That pain she must have been going through as well went straight through my heart. I was also crying, but not allowed to speak to Simone. Do you have any idea on how much that hurt us both? Anni you went to see Janice and her daughter often, and they both tried to help, and I was so grateful as it was my only link with Simone as to how she was. What she had been up to? Was she OK? They both were so wonderful. Janice, I am afraid, also had a big confrontation with you, as you seemed to be bragging about it, and just swaggered in and out of her house, as though nothing had happened, and somehow felt that Janice was going to give you sympathy.

Neither Janice nor I could understand why you thought like that. But of course Janice knew all about it, and was just as horrified as everyone else, perhaps even more so because she knew more, and had seen more, than most of my friends. Simone was everyone's concern, as what must have been going through her mind, nobody knows. Also she was listening to all the things you were saying and screaming about to everyone so what her thoughts must have been, I have no idea but it must have been so very confusing and damaging for her.

The pain that this caused me was beginning to make me ill. To hear Simone screaming in the background, crying hysterically that she wanted to come and see me was too much. Just take a minute and think how that would make you feel if you were at the end of that phone. We were so used to seeing each other so often, and spending so much time together which was all she had ever known. I was her second mum in a way and I had suddenly, for some reason, stopped seeing her. How she must have been hurting as well, but Anni you did not seem to care. It was as though, for the first time in your life, YOU were in control, and to this day I still believe that this was the main issue. You were in control of me, and Simone, and you felt good. I know you did because you told me and everyone else later.

The appointment for the mediation came through, but for some reason, Anni you said you could not make it, and changed the date, but I am afraid that the solicitors did not believe you and that made them cross. You were not working so what else were you up to? So I agreed with the solicitor that I would go on my own, and I was to meet a beautiful lady who had such understanding. I explained what had happened, what was happening now, and she said something, which I think was so very true. She felt that Anni you were extremely jealous of the relationship that I had with Simone, and she felt that mediation would not help as really Anni you just wanted to lay the ground rules down, and if I saw Simone, she would still be told off and possibly punished when she got home. We both felt that it would be extremely unfair to Simone, as why should she be punished for having a nice time, even if we had both abided by the rules, and she did not have coca- cola, or slept in my bed. Anni you had always said that when Simone came home from staying with me that "she was a little shit and uncontrollable and it takes you and Gray a week to sort her out afterwards." What the hell were you both doing to her when she got home, and why? Of course, yours and my ways of disciplining Simone were completely different but a relationship with a child is a bond, and discipline is only a small part. What was so wrong in her having a nice time with her nan?

So, what else could I do as speaking to you on the phone was so stressful and getting nowhere? So, I took some friends advice and wrote you a letter, which was unfortunately taken the wrong way. Anni, sometimes you find it hard to comprehend the contents, and you misunderstood the letter, so this infuriated you even more. I had showed it to Janice and Theresa before I sent it to you, as I did not want to put anything in there that would be hurtful, and they thought it was a lovely heartfelt letter, but Anni you just picked out a few things by highlighting lines and showed everyone, and was furious. And I mean furious.

By this time, I was just crying all the time, could not talk to people sometimes without bursting into tears, but my boss was giving me grief as well at work, as my figures where not up to standard, and I had told her all about what was happening at home. But this was still happening and it was a couple of months now since I had received that awful letter and not seen Simone. She was good and understanding for a while, but I felt that in the May I had to leave my job. I could not deal with both, as Anni you had come around to my house a couple of times, and on one occasion I had to throw you out. You came around for some bits of Simones that were at my house, and I thought this was an ideal opportunity to talk to you, which we did, and things were quite amicable until you said something so hurtful I could not contain myself. Apparently, I was "not needed any more" as Simone had another nanny now, Gray's mum, and so I was "surplus to requirements". For the first time in my life, I threw you out, and do you know what you did, you laughed, and laughed as you were going out the door. How could you have had so much spite and feelings in you? Well, Justin and Jackie, my next door neighbours, heard me slamming the door and came running. They had seen you come in to my house, so were a bit concerned, but I just burst into tears yet again. Actually I could not speak for a while. I was so hurt it was untrue. How could you say such things to me that I was "not needed any more"? They could not believe it either, so went back to their house to get the much needed wine! Bless them, they stayed with me for ages until I calmed down, but more was to follow.

I am not sure quite where, Anni, you were coming from in all of this; because you went on to tell me everything that you could think of to hurt me. You started off by saying that you were sending Simone to boarding school down in Devon, as you knew how much I would hate her going away, so this was one way of hurting me, and trust me that hurt. You told everyone, daddy, Edna, Robert, Elena, Janice, Emma and god knows who else, that Simone was actually at boarding school because I had gone up to Simone's school and tried to kidnap her, and the teachers had to ask me to leave, so in Simone's best interest, you would send her away. You said to me on the phone that Simone was there Monday to Friday and she was doing so well, playing loads of sports and that she loved it. You apparently went down to Devon at weekends to bring her back. Well, for a start I had never ever gone to Simone's school since this all happened, and anyone that knows me would also say that it is not something I would do. The school would also verify that this never happened, but the lies were only just beginning. A few months later you actually went round to everyone's house, Roberts, Janice's, Emma's and daddy's and said goodbye to them all, because now you, Simone and Gray were moving to Devon and you were not going to tell anyone your address, and you all were going to disappear. Actually, unbeknown to any of us, Simone never left her original school. I really was beside myself wondering if this was true or not, as the thought of you sending Simone to boarding school, and moving away without ever being able to see either of you was awful.

I just could not believe that this was happening, and could not concentrate on anything. I could not talk to anyone either without bursting into tears, so when friends or work colleagues asked me how things were, I just used to put my hand up to say not now, and they understood. The only people I could talk to were my close friends, and if half the conversation was me crying, then they were OK with that, and I did not feel stupid, because the tears would just not stop. It was so hard for anyone to understand exactly how I felt because thankfully, none of them have ever had to go through this, and I would not wish this on my worst enemy. But, unfortunately there are far too many other grandparents who are in the same position and it is awful. Our children seem to take great pleasure in letting us know that as grandparents, we have no rights, and don't seem to care what it is doing to us, or more importantly how it affects our grandchildren, their own children. I wish the law would hurry up and change. Actually, in desperation I phoned a wonderful organisation called the Grandparents Association[4] who listened, advised me that I was doing all that I could and the best thing to do was just to try and keep in contact as best I could with birthday cards, christmas cards etc.

A few days after the actual date that, Anni, you had given everyone for your move, daddy went round to your flat, just to see if you had really gone, and guess what, you all were still there. Even all your family and friends were as perplexed as me. Daddy and you started to be friends again then. But then you started to tell people that you all were about to move somewhere else, nearer home but again that was all lies. Then mother's day came, and you made an unannounced visit to your brother's house where you wanted to sort things out. Well, Robert and Elena had asked me over for the day, so when the banging on the door started, we all looked at each other, but it just went on and on, and you would not go away. So Robert opened the door and the screaming started. Then you noticed me, and all hell was let loose. The last thing Robert wanted was his neighbours to hear all the screaming that was going on, so he asked you to leave, which you eventually did, but came back a few days later but this time with Gray. According to you, Gray was going to sort him out, but he actually came into their house and shook Robert's hand and they had a discussion where Gray said that he was fed up with it all. I am sorry, but I have to say I feel he has played a big role in this separation and not helped the situation at all. He has a very big controlling influence on both you Anni and Simone.

A few months later, Gray or Anni, you shaved Simone's hair off completely, because of nits, which were a big problem I have to agree, but was that really necessary? The school straight away acted appropriately by informing social services, but I was blamed by you for this, big time, and for a long time. So, this was another reason why I could not see Simone, as I had apparently called social services and how awful I was. I cannot begin to tell you how many times I told you both that it was not me, but you were also telling everyone that social services had told you that it was me, which is something that they certainly would not have done. After a while Gray did give me permission to call social services which I did, and they confirmed to me that as far as they knew, Simone was still in her old school, and yes they were called because of the shaven head. They also confirmed that they would never tell me, or you who had made the original call if it was an independent person. They can only tell you if it is a doctor or a school. I found it very hard to imagine Simone with no hair, but daddy and

Janice saw her and said she wore a bandana on her head to cover it up. Simone said it was like Gray's now, but how was it received at school with her friends, as she looked like a little boy? But, of course, I did not know, as I was still not being allowed to see her.

But then a few months later, a change of heart, as apparently you both found out that it was not me who had called social services, and, apparently, it was one of your neighbours so I could now see Simone. Actually, Gray even apologised to me (as you did also) but that had hurt me to think that you even thought those thoughts, and however many times I told you that it was not me, did not seem to make any difference as it landed on deaf ears. Prior to this, Anni, you had come around one evening, and we had a long chat where we both cried, and you were beginning to come around to the idea of me seeing Simone, so my hopes were rising. You said that if I called you at the end of the week to let them know when it would be convenient for me to see Simone, because at this time, my old company that I had just left, asked me to go back as a contractor for six weeks, but it meant that I had to live away from home Monday to Friday.

So, with great excitement one Friday evening as I was driving home on the M25, I called to say that any time over the weekend would be fine and I was about to tell you how excited I was when there was a change of heart. Gray shouted at me and said that I could not see Simone under any circumstances, but while he was saying this, I could hear Simone in the background. God, I just burst into tears and how I managed to find somewhere to pull over I am not sure, as I could not see. The tears just flowed again. Oh, here we go again. The promises and the let downs were all too much. But then Anni you called me back, and said that it was Simone who did not want to see me now, as I was just aggravation and she did not want that. Anni you then passed the phone to Simone who just said "Nanny, I don't want to see you" and God how hurt I felt. I did not blame Simone at all because Simone had heard for the last six months all the screaming down the phone that Anni you had done, and the arguments that it caused with everyone including Gray. Because Simone was often there with you when you were expressing it all to everyone, so of course Simone was worried that it would all start up again. Anni you said, and I am sure you did, that you tried to tell Simone that you and I were now becoming friends again, but Simone was not sure. I had tried to say to you that you cannot just say to her that "mummy and nanny are now friends so things will be fine" as she had heard so much. What on earth had gone on and was going through her mind in all of this time? Six months is a very long time for a child to listen to anger, but also Anni you had told so many lies, what was Simone to believe? You cannot just turn back a clock with a child as they are too young to understand.

In all of this, I am not sure that Anni you gave any thought to what the long term effect would be on Simone, or me, but the lies continued. You had now made a file on me, which you loved showing to everyone. But included also in this file was a list of phone calls that I was meant to have made, up to 10 times a day apparently, and therefore I would not leave you alone, but while I was working away, strangely enough I got a frantic phone call from you. Gray had left you again, and he was going to come back and take all the furniture, because he had paid for it and would I help as you were so upset and needed me? Well, do you know I did. For some strange reason, and I am not sure why, I spent ages on the phone to you talking you through what you should do, that you would be OK and I would be back at the weekend, and would help. Am I mad, or what? But four phone calls later in the same day, you and Gray had worked it out so then everything was OK.

Strangely enough in either August or September 2003, I got another phone call from you to say that you had changed your mind and I could see Simone now, as it was not Gray stopping me seeing Simone, it was you. So the decision was yours, so could we make arrangements for Simone to come over to see me? Great, wonderful news until, in the next breath, your next words were, "can I ask you a favour?" Yes Anni you could, "well, I have seen this car that I would like to buy, and do you remember how much I have always wanted one of these, a Jeep, so could I borrow £500?" That was the last time I heard from you, because when I said "No", and suggested that you go to work and earn the money yourself, you screamed at me and put the phone down on me.

How strange, how could you think that blackmail was going to work in your favour? And then, after you had bought the car you could then change your mind and stop me seeing Simone again. I don't think so. You can not play with people's emotions, especially a child's. But I had to start getting on with my own life again now, as best I could. I still could not talk to people sometimes without bursting into tears, but occasionally I could and I was beginning to tell them what had happened and nobody could believe that something so awful was happening within a family, but unfortunately it does. Our family is not the only one to suffer this, it happens far too often. I was chatting to one of my work colleagues one day over a cigarette, when she told me that she had had to make a terrible decision, a few years ago and had walked out on her own children and she did not see them for four years. She was the first and only person that I have spoken to that I knew, who understood how I felt. It was such a relief, because she gave me hope. She is now reunited with her children, after a long and horrible struggle, but things had turned out well for her, so I have to believe that they will for me. I can't live any other way. It is the only way that I could move on, believing that things will be OK, and I trust that they will.

Hopefully soon, but at the time of writing this, I still have not seen you, Anni, since the summer of 2003, and my granddaughter since 17th February 2003, which is nearly two years ago. A very long time I can tell you. One way that I do try to keep in touch is at Christmas, Easter and on Simone's birthday when I will meet daddy who very kindly gives her a present from me that I have bought. I have no other way of doing it, but I cannot let Simone think that I have forgotten her, or that I do not care. That would be too awful.

How this will be resolved I have no idea but we have both learnt lessons from this I am sure. We tried talking to each other as you know, but we were unable to communicate, and neither of us seemed to listen properly to the other persons needs. But one thing I feel is that things may not change until, Anni you stop blaming everyone else in your life for your problems by taking responsibility for your own actions. This is something that you have always struggled with and you give the appearance that nothing bothers you, but of course inside, the most important part of a person, you do. Inside you are a very sensitive person, who takes things inwardly, but does not know how to express your feelings other than through frustration and anger. Maybe you felt that we all put you down in some way when you were going through your difficult times, and if that is so then I am sorry. That was not our intention as we all were only trying to help. You have such a lovely sensitive side and are a very caring person. You have always been there for your friends and this side of you is so much nicer than the side I have seen recently. Up until recently I was the only person who understood you. Why do you think I was always there for you? I have always known the good side of you, and I must admit a lot of people cannot see that. As your mum I have learnt to understand you because I have been through a lot of your difficulties with you. But now you have Gray in your life but I have to say that over-bearing control of Simone is, in my view, not the way to get the best out of her. She has to live her own life, as you both have done. Yes, we all make mistakes and I am sure I have made many as well. We all do, but perhaps it is now time to put the past behind us. I understand from daddy and a few friends of yours that you have less aggression inside of you, and are a much calmer person. I am glad that you are friends with daddy again as I think this is a big part of your own healing process.

I have also learnt a lot from this experience and I am sorry that it ever came to this and to this day I am not sure how it did. All I have ever tried to do is the best that I thought I could, that is what parents do. If you felt that I interfered then I am sorry but what else could I have done. You and I both agreed right from when Simone was born that you did not want her growing up struggling as you had done and asked for my help, which I freely gave. I have learnt a lot about life and I hope that I have always been kind, thoughtful, compassionate and understanding. But what I have also done is be true to myself and I have tried to be strong throughout but it has not always been possible.

So, I have gradually started to move on again. The contract from my old company, which was originally for six weeks was extended as things kept going wrong, so my work colleague, Peter, and I had to stay down at our head office, where, because of the travelling on the M25 on a Monday morning can be so horrendous, they put us up in a hotel. We lived out of a hotel for six and a half months, as the project was just not working properly, and it went on and on. But in some ways this was good for me, because we were so busy, and we worked such long hours, it kept my mind off my problems. I told Peter what was happening at home, because I was still getting the occasional phone call, and, of course, this would sometimes reduce me to tears again, and he was brilliant, and so were my other work colleagues down there. Actually, I never told some of them what was happening at home, because I found it hard to talk about it still, and it seemed easier not to say anything. We did have some laughs amongst us, and they were a good crowd, which made the separation from home so much nicer. But, of course, I came home every Friday night for the weekend, and usually this brought all the emotions back, so Monday to Friday I was OK as we were so busy, but Saturday and Sunday I often went to pieces again, as it brought all the memories back again. What an odd existence I was living, when I think about it.

But, life at home was carrying on as normal as it could be. Janice I would normally see at the weekend, and we would go out. Or I would go to see other friends and socialise, but one thing I was missing enormously was my spiritual circle that I belonged to. We meet every other Monday evening, at Cathy's house but because I was away Monday to Friday I could not attend and I was missing this. But, when I was working away, I was not seeing or hearing my spirit guides nearly as much as I used to, but this was because I was often tired, and my mind was on what was going on at work. So in some ways it had been 'put on hold'. This, I was to learn, was quite normal, and it would come back (and it certainly has).

We did do a couple of Charity Fund Raising days when some of us did tarot readings, astrology charts and I did angel card readings. These were great and very uplifting for all of us, not only the readers but the guests, who walked away very happy, and usually inspired. One of the days we did was for one of our circle members Debbie, to raise funds for her to have a new start after her divorce. Another day was for another circle member Sharon to help her raise money for her life's work 'The Children of the Nile' in Egypt.

A beautiful moment

But, now that I have written of the terrible events which have happened to me, about my separation from Simone, I can now tell you about something which also happened which is beautiful, and it occurred one very special evening, before I started working away, as you would now, I hope, understand more why this happened.

One night in circle, about a month after the last day that I had seen Simone, when the pain was so very raw, and the hurt so very deep, we went into a meditation. Sharon and I just sat together quietly, holding hands and we began to see the most amazing colours, and had such a wonderful feeling, it was like a beautiful glow. We were both so very still, and could not move because we knew that my angel was with me, wrapping her arms around me, giving me a beautiful gentle cuddle just as she had done at the Challis Well. Then my angel very, very gently put a tear on my cheek, which was so so beautiful, and I could just feel this tear, and we were told that she was feeling my pain as well. Oh god, what a beautiful moment, and how honoured I felt. There are no words that I could say that would describe it. When I came out of this meditation, I could not speak, and tears just rolled down my cheeks. I felt so truly honoured - to feel such love is very special to me.

Angels come to you in so many different ways, to everyone in all walks of life, but mine comes in person - how lovely to have been chosen.

These experiences I have had with my angels are very special as they have brought so much into my life. They really have kept me sane and they have enriched my life and been such a comfort to know that I am not alone. This in some ways has given me strength and given me the feeling that all will be well. By learning to trust and knowing that I am being looked after by not only my angels but also by other spirit guides, has given me such peace inside. I have learnt to stop struggling and fighting with all that is going on around me. Everything will be resolved one day soon I hope but, until that time comes - when the "bigger picture" is revealed - I know that I can enjoy all that I have in a much more fulfilled way. The pleasures in life are to be enjoyed and the love that I have inside me I can now share with everything that I do. Love to me is what makes the world go around and I am so lucky to have received and shared so much love

I do hope...

At this present time, I still have not seen Simone, or heard from you Anni and I have to get on with my life as still such beautiful things are happening. Robert and Elena have been a wonderful blessing, and little James is growing up fast and is a lovely boy who will be starting school soon, and I enjoy his 'little' company, and theirs, as often as I can. They both still find it hard to understand how I feel or why I still want to restore harmony with you as they have seen some of the hurt that I have gone through, and are so angry. I feel so sad that you both have not spoken to each other for such a long time. Life is too short.

When you both moved out of the cottage I thought it may be time to find a smaller cottage but could not find one that I liked. I had seen various cottages but I had not yet put my house on the market. But one night 'they' showed me a picture of a lady walking along the path leading to my cottage so I thought that she was going to be the person who would buy it, so *now* must be the right time to move. So I phoned an agent on a Friday, and then over the weekend I went to see a new cottage that had just come on the market and fell in love with it. I can only describe it as home. I just wanted to sit down in it, so put in an offer knowing that I was putting my house on the market the following day. Then on the Monday morning the agent arrived and I was shocked. She was the lady I had been 'shown' in the picture earlier so obviously it was time to move on. I now live in this lovely 600 year old cottage which is home.

Janice my closest friend, I miss enormously as she has moved to Spain now, and has bought a house out there. I have been to see her often, and we talk on the phone as often as we can, but it is not the same. She felt she had to move on, as we all do, and loves it out there. I have to agree that the move was so right for her. As she says, maybe she will stay for ever, or may be she will move on to another place in a few years time, but it is right for her now. Maybe she will come back here to live, who knows. She does miss her family a lot, but they have been to see her over there, and now say that it is great that she is living there as they can have cheap holidays! She will be coming home for short holidays here as often as she can.

Theresa and I still are very much in touch and we still tell each other, and ponder over, all that we see, or feel, or hear from our 'friends' and she has grown from these experiences, the same as I have. She is teaching now, but her life is about to move on, in probably a very special way, which we both look forward to!

Cathy, Theresa, Sharon and the other Circle members are still very special friends, and always will be. We have a Circle meeting every other Monday, which I so enjoy. We also socialise an awful lot together which is brilliant, and a few new people Francis, Cathy A, Ingrid and Janine who have recently joined us, so I look forward to working with them as well. We are off to Glastonbury soon again, and I really am looking forward to it, because this time it will be my opportunity for me to say 'thank you' to my angels. This time I will in my own way, put my own arms around my angels, as last year I was honoured again and met my angel when I went to The Challis Well. That really is a very special garden for me.

Lesley and Julie I see as well, as often as I can, but Lesley has moved on to a lovely new life and lives in a beautiful village in Majorca, but, hey, what a lovely opportunity for me to have great weekend breaks. I have been to see her and I am sure I will visit again soon.

My old work colleagues I still see on a regular basis, which is great and we still discuss our lives and work over a pint (or in my case a glass of wine) followed usually by a late night meal. Great evenings with great company.

Mandy, Greta, Janet, Molly, Sharon, Karen and all my other friends, I see as often as I can, which varies from month to month as we all lead quite busy social lives, and after all these years, still enjoy their company as much as ever.

Daddy and Edna have moved away, but we are in touch and speak on the phone, or I will meet daddy to give him a present to give to Simone. He now sees you Anni and Simone, and Simone often stays with him for a few days in the school holidays, which I am so pleased about. He is one of my only contacts on how Simone is doing. Anni, you and your dad are now friends again which I am so pleased about. You and Gray are now working together running a house clearance business, and I wish you both well, and hope it is successful. But for some strange reason Anni you are still telling a lot of lies about me, how you bumped into me and all that I have said to you. Sad really, as these are completely untrue as you know. Your cousin Adam came over from Australia recently to see all of us, and we all hoped that the importance of family life would have been re-kindled in you when he came to stay with you. Your family life used to be important, and I know how you and Simone enjoyed his visit, as he did. Hopefully the healing process you are beginning to go through with your friendship with your dad will be the beginning.

And myself, well I am still living in my lovely cottage which I adore, living life as best and to the full, but unfortunately recently I learnt that my skin cancer is active again, which I must say devastated me as it has been nine years since I last had to have a mole removed. This time it was not only another mole on my leg that had to go, but a 'bubble' as I call it on my face, so this has been a lesson to me that the sun and I really do not go together. But, I have dealt with it, and decided that hats will be a big feature for me in the summers, along with long skirts and tops with sleeves. Quite feminine actually. But what is far more important is that I have the rest of my health and a positive attitude and certainly will not give in to it.

One problem I have is how will I recognise Simone as it has been such a long time since I have seen her? She now has adult teeth which will have altered her face, of course, and no hair. Every time I go shopping, I look at so many children wondering if it is Simone and it hurts. I have this vision that I may bump into her and it could go either way. She may be so nervous at seeing me that she may shy away, or we may just run into each others arms and hug and kiss. She is only a child and it has been such a long time. I am sure that we will recognise each other, but the circumstances of the reunion are unknown to me at this time. What I hope I will not do is cry, but I know I will. I will cry with joy and sadness but I don't want to hurt you Simone as you may be confused on how to react. As long as you know that I love you and always will, then that is all that matters.

My spiritual journey, which has not only been amazing, is growing all the time and I do not honestly know what I would have done without it. It is so lovely to know that we are all not alone, and I look forward to learning all that I can, reading all that I can, and talking to others about it, as it is a wonderful gift, and a joy to have. I am looking forward to the rest of my life's journey.

I went recently to a spiritualist evening in our local village hall. This is something I have never done before and I so very nearly stood up when a man was asking how they have developed their knowledge, and the two mediums said that it had started in childhood for them and that was quite usual. Well to me that was not how it had really started for me, as I may have had it in childhood but I certainly was not aware of it. I so wanted to tell this man that it can happen and develop at any time in your life, and that he should pursue it whenever he could. We all have the potential and, Robert and Anni, I know that you both in the past have had brief experiences and if you want to develop this, then please do talk to me or someone about it. Simone I hope will develop her psychic abilities, which I know she has, later in her life.

Recently, something happened that is tinged with sadness. One of my circle friends, Theresa's husband Adonis, died suddenly at the age of 39. It was a terrible shock and tragedy to us all but it has brought back so many emotions to me that I thought I had buried. Adonis dying has been a big shock and Theresa is part of our circle, so a few days after his death we had a healing circle for her and during this circle something amazing happened. One of our circle members Anthony came through to me and asked me to say that he wished to be remembered and he was here with us tonight and wanted to send his love to Theresa. I passed on this message and we all thought it strange because he was not here but he had always loved to be a part of the circle, but had not attended for various reasons for some time. Well, Sharon another circle member picked up on this as she had been concerned about him for a few days and not seen him. She went the next day with a friend to his house, only to find that he had passed away in his sleep in his bed a few days previously. So he *had* been with us but in *spirit*. That was a very powerful experience and I feel very honoured that Anthony chose me to pass his message on. Both were such lovely men. Sharon was a friend so it was a message to her as well. Theresa did find this powerful message a comfort and clarification as she had experienced communication, through various ways, from Adonis. It proved to her and us that there is 'life after death'.

All I can do now is wait and hope, which is, and has been, so very hard. Patience is probably one of the hardest lessons I have had to learn, and God how hard that is. But I do have a wonderful thing called 'trust' and I know that when the time is right, Simone and I will be reunited. But I hope to be able to tell you very soon, how wonderful it is to have her back in my life. The future with you, Anni, I hope will also be repaired one day soon too. How or when I have no idea, but time is a very funny thing.

God bless you all

Love mum xx

P.S. I know this letter may be long but I just want you all to know, my children as well as my grandchildren, how lovely it is having you in my life, and you all have taught me so much about life and I am still learning every day. What I would like to do now is pass on to you and others in the next part, some of my knowledge and thoughts about life that I have learnt over time. I hope that you will find inspiration within these words which will help you live a very long and happy life. Some may be relevant to you others will not be, so please take from them what you wish.

Second Edition
I have some good news – the future

Since I first published my book, some wonderful things have happened. The timing of these events is actually quite strange! It proves to me that everything is 'meant to be'.

You see, the day I received my first copy of my book in my hands, in the afternoon I got a sudden phone call, completely out of the blue, to say my granddaughter Simone wanted to come and see me. Could she come round in half an hour? I suddenly cried, panicked, ran around the house not knowing what to do as I was completely in shock. Anni did not know about the book; how had this come about? What would we say, how would she feel, what did she look like as we had not seen each other for over two years. Then I thought she would probably be just as nervous as me, so I went outside to greet her so she would not feel uncomfortable. Oh, the joy it brought to both of us is beyond words.

The car arrived and we waved at each other which broke the ice and then she was grinning from ear to ear. I could see she was a little nervous but she had her school uniform on so I started asking her very casually about her badge on her jumper and she just giggled. She giggled for an hour, happily chatted, wrote me a lovely letter and I wrote her one back. And then she was gone.

The tears then started, but they were different. They were joyous tears but also sad tears. I knew she was OK. Because it was sudden I had no time to think about things (which was good,) but then I began to wonder why. After all this time, what had suddenly changed Anni's and my granddaughter's minds? To this day I have never asked as in some ways it did not seem to matter. I think somehow 'they' had something to do with it as the timing was unbelievable! She wanted to come back soon so I told Simone that she could come around anytime she wanted too, it was up to her. She knew that I still loved her and that was all that mattered.

But then I did not hear from her because Anni said we had to first re-build our relationship again with each other and I did agree. Our relationship had altered and had become strained because of the hurt on both sides. But Anni and Gray then read my book and began to reflect, so we meet for lunch on quite a few occasions and I did not mention once about seeing Simone as I felt that this would come later. But I learnt there was another agenda.

I must say the meetings were quite difficult for us both. Earlier in the year she had fallen out with her dad again, and they have now not seen each other for a long time. So much had happened but our bonding was beginning to get easier between us when things took a sudden turn. Anni suddenly announced that she and Gray had decided to get married but none of the family was invited to the wedding. It was just to be the three of them plus friends but only two friends came as witnesses as no other friends or even Gray's family turned up! A friend told me the date, time and venue as I could not let the occasion go by without seeing both of them. So I hid and watched from a local multi-storey car park which over looks the venue. If anyone had seen me, they must have wondered what on earth was going on as I kept moving my spot as I did not want to be noticed. How could I have explained that I was not allowed to my own daughter's wedding? That hurt but Anni and Simone looked lovely But more was to come. I got a phone call from Anni on my mobile a few minutes after her wedding to tell me she had tied the knot, and a sarcastic "thanks for being there". Her dad also got a phone call from her to say she had got married and awaited a cheque for £5,000, which she assumed she would receive because we both had given her brother that amount when he got married, so where was hers? So having thought things might have altered following our relationship building, things obviously had not changed AT ALL!

Two weeks later, my sister was coming over from Australia on a whirlwind whistle stop tour of England and of course wanted to see everyone. So we arranged to meet all the family on Sunday, but it would have been very awkward if Gray, Anni and Simone had been there, so we agreed to meet separately in a pub for lunch the next day.

Oh, what a beautiful and wonderful day. My sister and brother-in-law stayed with me overnight and we drove to the pub with great excitement but also anticipation. Would they turn up, would she create a scene, would they bring Simone, we had no idea. Anni can be very unpredictable. But we need not have worried because suddenly little Simone was running out of the car with the biggest smile on her face I have ever seen.

We ran straight into each others arms and cuddled. She then sat with me all the time, I played with her on the swings and we laughed and laughed for 3 beautiful hours. We kept whispering to each other "I love you" but then we had to leave, as my sister was visiting other relations and the time had run out. When we said goodbye Simone just kept asking me over and over again "Nanny, when will I see you again?" I promised it would not be long and told her that I would arrange something with her mum.

I honestly thought that this would happen, because things had gone so well. But, it didn't continue for long as apparently regular visits were still not allowed. Those words "Nanny, when will I see you again" have begun to haunt me, as I cannot keep my promise. My daughter, her mum, and her new husband have gone back to playing 'the control' game again. But, some months later Simone and I were 'allowed' to see each other again at Christmas for a few hours and we had a wonderful time playing games, giggling, chatting and the smile on her face was beautiful. I gave her some presents and I learnt that she is happy and doing well at school, and loves sport. There is still an awful lot about her life I don't know because three years in a child's life is a long time, and we have to gradually re-build our relationship and get to know each other again. Children change such a lot in their growing years but in some ways that does not matter. I now know, without doubt, that when she is older she will be able to make her own choices but at least for now she knows that I love her. She was so little when this all started and too young to understand then.

All I do know is that I continue to 'trust' and that one day soon regular contact will be established, but for the moment I cannot, and will not; play with a child's emotions. It seems too often that children become pawns within a relationship.

I have since become a volunteer for The Grandparents' Association and what I hear on the other end of the telephone is astounding. It seems that so many other grandparents have no contact either and is becoming far more common than I ever imagined, and my experiences are nothing compared to others.

It is not just grandparents that are separated from their grandchildren. Lone fathers, lone mothers, brothers and sisters can and do experience just the same feelings. Surely no one has the right to play with other people's emotions, especially a child's. They are often the innocent victims.

I have been very lucky and seen my granddaughter briefly but others are not so lucky. Regular contact with Simone is still not allowed, only occasionally, but in time I am sure it will be. But for other grandparents, life still continues to be heart breaking. No one, unless they have experienced something like this, can ever imagine or feel their pain. People often think that this sort of thing will never happen to them – but unfortunately it does and far too often. My heart is singing but other hearts are still crying.

Book Two

My thoughts for you about life

To be a star, you must shine your own light,
follow your own path and don't worry about the darkness,
for that is when stars shine the brightest
-unknown-

Chapter 1
Your journey and who goes with you

To handle yourself, use your head,
To handle others, use your heart

Anon

Sometimes we come to a stage in life where we begin to think about our own lives and life in general. Some may feel that the time has come to move on in some way. Others will never question things in their life. But we can all learn new things at what ever stage we are at, and for those of you that want to I hope you can pick up some ideas and suggestions within these chapters which may help you in some way. Some may be relevant to you others will not be, so please take from them what you wish.

I first started to think about my own life when someone said to me that "you come into this life on your own and you leave on your own, but who you meet along the way, and what you do with your life, is up to you".

It has taken me years to realise the truth behind this statement and when I first heard it, it upset me. I don't like to think I am *alone*, and it made me feel very alone. Then my thoughts ran deeper. Yes, I am an individual, a lone person and as an individual, only *I* know what my whole life has been like. It is therefore a lonely journey and while

112

others can view me from the outside, only I know what's going on *inside*.

This is the way I view life as I now realise we are alone throughout our lives because no one else experiences our emotions. Yes, our family and friends keep us company on our journey and all play an important role, but only YOU know how you feel about your life experiences and which of them have made the most impact on your life.

We are becoming more aware of our multi cultural society, different faiths and traditions, but whatever culture you were born into, you learnt by the examples set by your family, and your upbringing, and this will have an impact on you and the way you lead your life. For many of you, your parents are your most important teachers and role models but they will never know *everything* about you.

Each of us meets different experiences as we grow up and if you have brothers and sisters, none of you will see your upbringing as the same. Yes, certain things happen to you all, but you will each have different relationships within your family. You will each have your own lessons to learn and you will all be different personalities. There might be one of you in the family who is very loving and giving, another may need a lot of attention, another may be more successful than the others, and this all affects how you see yourself and others in later life.

Each experience you share with the people in your life will be different. For example, if someone has been through a trauma or something exciting with a particular friend or relation, then it may develop a special bond between you. It can also help you to understand each other which is very important and part of accepting people just as they are. We each experience different events and emotions at different times in our lives and only we ourselves know what they are, and what effect they have had on us.

We each have our own personalities from birth, our own abilities, qualities and ideas on what we want from life but some of the experiences we go through and the people that we meet along our journey can be a major influence on us and help to shape us as a person.

Just think about some of the events in your life, which may have been happy or sad, and the people who shared them with you. Have you ever been on your own when something happy has happened? I bet you wanted to share the experience with lots of people, but if it was a difficult or sad experience, then you may have kept it bottled up inside you for a long time. Sometimes, if you can share your feelings when you feel stronger it helps you to move on in life and by sharing them; you can also start to heal.

Each person sees something different in an individual and can bring out their best or worse qualities, and vice versa. Sometimes when we meet someone for the first time, we instantly feel that we will get on well together - others take longer to bond with. Some people we may never bond with as our personalities clash.

Once we get older and can look back on our life, we realise how important our childhood is. It may have been a very positive experience or a negative one, but it is the only grounding to life we have and our values in future life tend to be based on what we learn as children.

A simple example: I was brought up to have meals together as a family around the dining room table – it was an important part of family life. I always brought my children up to have their meals at the table too (albeit sometimes in the kitchen) but the concept is the same. Meal times are when you can get together and share the day's experiences - such intimate family times help to shape the person we are. It shows we are interested in each other and we care. Spending quality time with your children is important; it can help with your child's confidence.

As we grow older, and especially if we have children, we seem to view the issues in our life differently and the values that we hold sometimes change. How many people say 'if only I had known that earlier in life?' We go through childhood, pass through our teens and into our 20's, then 30's, 40's and 50's and so on - growing and learning every step of the way. Each stage, whether it has good or bad experiences can be reflected on after we have worked through some of the issues, and in looking back we can see that we have possibly learnt something. Not *possibly*, we *have*. We learn from every experience we have.

An example of this is when I was at college doing a counselling degree; I was asked to draw a picture of my life. Well, I have never been a very good artist and found this idea quite difficult as I could not see the point; what would this tell me? But I realised afterwards there was a reason. So I drew a river, and along the two banks either side I flagged the big events which had happened. Some of them were good, some not so good, but a lot of the time, I found myself clinging onto the side of the river, and then gradually being brought back to the middle. Again and again I found myself in the middle of the river. The further I moved along my journey, the clearer I could see the end, which I saw as the opening to the ocean. I was nearly there and felt that soon there would be no need to cling onto the river banks as I would be out into the open sea.

Looking at my picture I realised my life was, perhaps, already mapped out before I was even born, and my journey was not always easy but I was getting there. Now I am 'going with the flow', and it is wonderful and in so many ways easier - I am not struggling, I just trust, accept and let things happen. I believe we all have our lives mapped out for us, and we all have 'free will' to make as many choices as we want. Sometimes opportunities come into our lives and we grasp them, other times they slip through our fingers but I believe that in the end, we are all brought back to the life that we were meant to lead. Life is to be enjoyed. No one said it was going to be easy but if you can be positive, and learn from each lesson your life will improve.

Activity

Why don't you write down all the big events in your life and see how your journey has been?

This activity you could do on your own or with friends or family. You could write or draw your life in a way you feel comfortable with. For example, some people in college drew trees, and the apples or leaves on the tree were the events in their life. Some were half way up, others were nearly at the top, and one person felt that she was still down the bottom. State the events in your life. When you have finished, take a look and see where you are now. How do you feel about it? Is there a pattern running through, or is each experience different? Can you see anything emerging and where are you along your river or up your tree? Is your journey getting you to where you want to be? If you have done it with other people, talk to them and share it

One of the lessons to learn in life is how to let go and move on. It means accepting whatever comes along and putting it to good use, and learn from it. Sometimes we hold on to things for too long, and this is when pressure can sometimes happen. Pressure then leads to stress. Sometimes when people suffer, they can spend the rest of their lives feeling sorry for themselves. Others, who may have had a similar experience, move on. They are the ones that look on life positively despite having shed just as many tears.

We hear of people who have a fatal illness, doing marvellous things right up to the last minute, because they decide to live the life they have remaining, to the full. So how we *think* is important. In a similar way, if we want to better ourselves, then we can. If we want to stay in the same old comfortable routine, then that is fine, but if you are not happy with that old routine, you can change it, even if it is a big step to take. Isn't it better to move on to the things that make you happy rather than stay in a place of unhappiness? This can be a difficult thing to do but hopefully as you read on you may find different ideas and suggestions which will help.

Sometimes people seem to go through life feeling guilty about something, or jealous or angry. This is not healthy. If you look at the underlying cause of these emotions you may find the cause is possibly resentment. Why are you jealous of someone? Why are you continually angry with someone, or everybody? Of course anger is a natural feeling but if we can learn to deal with it in a different way by perhaps punching a pillow, or imagine talking to that person in the mirror, it can relieve the frustration, rather than expressing it verbally. Unless you address this, the pattern of emotions will repeat itself; you will just create more and more anger and will hurt yourself far more than anyone else. Holding onto resentment will prevent you moving on.

If you feel guilty about something that you may have done years ago, then try and release that guilt, by saying to yourself that OK, it happened, but it is now time for me to start moving on and not to look back all the time. This sort of feeling will not go away over night. Once you start to recognise that you are feeling these thoughts (and really, they are just thoughts) then your mind will start to become clearer, and you may find that a whole weight will be lifted from your shoulders, and it will be a relief.

Activity

Why don't you ask yourself some of these questions?
Write down your answers on a separate sheet of paper

Why am I choosing to be angry all the time?
What am I doing to keep creating situations that make me angry?
Is this the only way I can react to situations?
What signals am I giving out to attract others that irritate me?

Why am I jealous of someone?
What is it that I am actually jealous of?
Why do I feel that if I had something it would make me feel better?
Why do I still feel guilty about something that happened in the past?
Then ask yourself
How can I deal with this better?
Perhaps by writing the answer down it will help

Anger is only one letter short of danger.

If you point a finger at someone, three fingers will be pointing back to you!

If someone betrays you once, it is their fault, if they betray you twice, it is your fault.

Along your life's journey there will be things that happen and people you meet that either block your way or lift you along to a better place.

Take the workplace for example. Often, it is the people at work that make or break you in your career. If you love your job and are energised by it, then you will attract positive people around you who will then, in turn, probably encourage you to go further. If they can see the buzz you create, then that becomes infectious. Positive people attract positive things.

Professional sports people, for example, are so positive about their goals in life and are determined to reach the top that people around them believe in them. They are focused and have determination. Sometimes they are naturally talented like some footballers or tennis players. But others, although dedicated to success and to being top, have to train extremely hard. *But one thing they all have is positive thinking.* They do not reach the top of their profession by dwelling on their last bad result, they have to move on.

If you lose your job, some people find it can be the best thing that has ever happened and they find inspiration and a chance to do the very thing they have always wanted to. Others, however, give up. Sometimes a change can be good and life changing but we don't always realise this at the time.

A good example of this is two friends of mine who worked in the City. One was a stockbroker and the other a manager. The stockbroker felt that broking was all he knew and he could not possibly do anything else as he could not adapt. He went into deep depression as he felt he couldn't maintain the family's very good lifestyle, and unfortunately committed suicide. The other friend got a job driving a lorry, as he felt he had to do something to continue to support his family, so he turned his hand to something else. He did not particularly like his new role at first, but he then went on to become a manager again as the company saw his potential.

There are people you meet along your journey who are either a help or hindrance. But it may take you a while to work out which of these they are going to be. For instance, perhaps if you are in a difficult relationship, it may be that the person you are with is the same type of person that you have been used to all your life. For example some people who have had a traumatic childhood (possibly abused or experienced violence) attract a partner who abuses them. If that is you, then the only way to get off of this roller coaster is to change. It may be that you feel comfortable with this type of person at first, but then when events start to happen, you are frightened. But you *can* change the situation despite it being a very hard thing to do, and you may need to look within yourself as to why you are being treated this way. This may take time but once you recognise that you are not responsible for these circumstances then it is time for you to break away and attract into your life something or someone new. Some people don't feel they deserve better, but we **all** deserve the best that we can have.

A break-up of a relationship which can be a parting, divorce or a death can be, and normally is, a very painful experience. The effect on us and the way we cope can be very different and some people move on quicker than others.

Others never get over it, and often feel bitter or resentful, and even suicidal. Others involve the children in the disputes that are going on, and not only hurt themselves, but hurt the children too - unintentionally, of course, but in their bitterness, they feel it is one way to hurt their partner. Sometimes, the relationship breaks down and it is a mutual decision, so there is no bitterness, and it is easier for people to then move on, in time. When it is a sudden 'out of the blue' break-down, or parting, it can be quite a shock and may take longer.

But, if you can work through it and learn to forgive, it can help you to feel good and by forgiving yourself or someone else is a wonderful lesson to learn. It is never easy when children are involved but how WE deal with it, can make it easier for them.

So life's journey takes us through rough and smooth relationships and along the way we find people who are supportive and others who are not. As a woman I have found that sometimes talking with a friend, sometimes for hours on end, helps enormously. Men sometimes do not find it so easy to talk. Some men, if they are open to their feminine side, will talk and some men do cry which I think is lovely, and they are not afraid to show that they do have feelings; we all do but we can't always show it. I am sure *most* of us want at the end of the day, the same things. To be loved, and to love in return. To have a companion to share common interests with; someone to tell what your day has been like, to have a friend or to be part of a couple; to have a family and to have someone to come home to; to have cuddles, to express and release our feelings (sometimes through sex) and just to even hold hands with the one we love; but what we all want eventually is to find the perfect relationship.

Is there such a thing? I am sure there is. I think most of us want to believe that there is. We don't all feel like that which is fine but we must not feel that to meet the perfect partner will be the answer to our happiness. We have to love ourselves first on the *inside* and then when we do meet a partner (if that is what we want) we have to work at it. We have to accept our partners as they are, we cannot change them. This is the person that we originally fell in love with, when we didn't see their faults, and we accepted and loved them just as they were. Some couples may find that with time their relationship gets to the point of just being a habit and they are just existing with one another - the spark that they first felt has died. Well for most it doesn't last forever, but sometimes it can, but it changes into another feeling like contentment. People do change, but if we try, if we work at it, and if we want it, WE CAN change it and put some excitement back in.

Creating excitement does not have to be expensive, but a little surprise can go a long way. A spontaneous gesture can be wonderful. It brings excitement and interest back into a relationship. An evening out, possibly a meal, just the two of you, can be quality time and it shows that you care. It does not have to be an expensive meal, or if you don't go out, you can spend the evening on your own together. It sometimes is just the thought that can create such pleasure. I can hear some of you saying 'but it is such an effort' or 'I have not got the time' or even 'I can't be bothered'. A little bit of effort goes a long, long way and can be worth it as creating excitement needs only a little bit of imagination. I'll give you an example of something I did when I was going out with a partner. One day I came across his car, parked outside his workplace. So I wrote a note, quite a sexy one and it was raining, so I found a plastic bag and put the note inside and popped it under his windscreen wipers so that when he came out of work he would see it. Well, he drove his car at very high speed, turned up on my doorstep and just carried me upstairs. He said he found this gesture exciting and aroused emotions in him once he discovered it was not a parking ticket! I left quite a few notes after that, but never to quite the same effect. Also rather than just giving, I leave presents or sweets sometimes for my grandson to find perhaps at Easter dotted around the garden, under bushes, behind plants and he loves this. So you see, these gestures have never been expensive but create such fun.

So many couples seem to get into such a rut, and it is hard for them to pull out of it, or even do not want to. This is such a shame as at the beginning of the relationship, maybe many years ago, they would have been head over heels in love.

Activity

*Why not try to sit down together and just talk about your feelings. Perhaps **separately** over the next week, make a list of five to ten things that you want out of the relationship. Make a list of all the things that you love about each other and some of the things that have changed over the years. I know one couple that every now and then, write a list of what they expect and want from their relationship.*

The reason that they do this is because over the years, relationships and situations do change, and people change, but their commitment to each other has never wavered - well yes sometimes, and that is why they do this exercise – it brings them both back to being in the same place. Take your time writing your list and then arrange some quality time when there is just the two of you, and spend the evening discussing each and every one of them.

This often leads to other issues coming out, some may be painful ideas if someone is unhappy, but surely isn't it better to talk about problems and feelings, than to just hide them?. That is when things start to go wrong. Be respectful to each other

Some people in a partnership or marriage talk about 'I love them, but...' and then think that they can change that person into who they want them to be. Sorry, but no. No one can change a person, only they can do this themselves, and only if they want to. Maybe it is something insignificant that you may want to change, or it may be something like one of you taking a lot of time out of your week together. A good example is someone who is passionate about sport. They may want to watch *all* sports on the television, go to support their club or team and play themselves. But this could be a brilliant opportunity for you to usefully spend time away from each other and make it quality time for *you*. He or she is having their own quality time so why shouldn't you? Accept that it happens and join in or plan something for you and you may find that the resentment you may hold will go!

Everyone needs a little time to themselves, even if it is just for a few hours each week. Never feel guilty about quality time for you. It gives you space, away from a lot of the pressures and it is surprising how it will make you feel, more relaxed and refreshed. So many people think that they don't have time to do this, but what they don't realise is how much you will benefit from it. You will actually be less stressed and have more time as your thoughts and actions will be more relaxed and therefore you will actually achieve more.

Chapter 2
You and your purpose

You see things and say "why" But I dream things that never were; and I say "why not" – George Bernard Shaw 1856 – 1950

Have you ever wondered what your purpose is in life? Do you just accept that this is your life and never question why you are here, or what it is that you want? You may just plod along doing the best you can and perhaps dream that one day things will change or you may be very happy with the way things are and your life is good. I think most people have a dream of what life could be like if they are a little unhappy with things in their life, but perhaps we could make that dream come true. We all sometimes dwell too much on the negative things in our lives while we should be SHOUTING about all the positive things. From what we see in the news and newspapers, we seem in general, to focus more on what is wrong in the world and sometimes the good news gets put to the back. I think we should praise ourselves and others for the good that we do, and for our achievements that have been a success. We only seem to do this occasionally. Why don't we do it more often?

So what is your purpose? We all have a purpose but it is not always clear to some. Sometimes and very often it isn't until we are older that we realise what our purpose is. Some people never find out because they don't want to. Just take a minute to think about something. Why do

125

Before I Get Old and Wrinkly!

you think you are here on this earth and for what reason? Now that is a very big question so take your time thinking about it. We may never know all the answers but perhaps some of you may like, at a later stage, to read and learn more on this subject in which ever way you feel is right to do so. Others will never question it. Both are OK as we are all different. But for now, are you getting from your life all that you want and deserve, or are you just plodding and accepting? Some people put up blocks and we often know what is not working and we know what we want, yet we don't know how to move forward. Sometimes we haven't got the faintest idea of what is stopping us moving forward, and finding our true purpose, but maybe we have to acknowledge a block and let it go. There could be a number of reasons why we don't do this but, unless you address this issue, there will always be a block. Once you do address it, you will regain a sense of purpose. Once you have a sense of purpose, it will give more meaning to your life.

So what is it that you want to make yourself feel? More fulfilled maybe? You may be in a wonderful position to have achieved all that you can and are happy with yourself and your life. I hope that most of you are, but some people are still dreaming and wondering. What have you achieved and why don't you tell others more often? What can you still do to reach your goals? If you want to do this little activity where you can see your dreams and your achievements on a piece of paper, it may help to establish in your mind what it is you want out of life, and will help you focus on your dream. You can reach that dream and turn it into reality.

Activity

1. When I daydream about the future, what do I see myself doing?
2. What do I really want more than anything?
3. How will I feel?
4. If I had the freedom that I didn't need to earn money, what would I do with my time?
5. What is much better in my life now than before?
6. I believe about myself that I am.........? (list your qualities)
7. What does a perfect day in your life look like?
8. What has given me the most pleasure?
9. What has been my greatest success?
10. If I could have one wish and knew that it would **not** fail, what would it be?
11. What have I learnt in my life so far?
12. At the end of my life, I want my family/ friends/children to remember me in the following ways – list them
13. What have I contributed to the world?
14. My life will have been a waste if I?
15. What steps can I make to achieve my desires?
16. What makes me happy/feel good/ fulfilled?
17. How will I feel if I can achieve what I want?
18. Have you started to experience any of those feelings?
19. What action plan can I put into place for me to achieve my desires?
20. Do I have any regrets?

Chapter 3
You can change

"Start by doing what is necessary, then what is possible and suddenly you are doing the impossible"
St. Francis of Assisi

You can change your life if you are willing to change your thinking.

Many people feel that they have no time to think clearly about their life – let alone finding the time to do something about it. But I think you will find that it really is worth taking the time. There are various ways in which we can change, or change our circumstance which can help us to live a happier easier life. Some people even believe that stress is good for them and they are not working hard enough or achieving something unless they are stressed. To some it has become a way of life!

You may have begun to realise that there is a part of you that would like to change, but you may not know how to or you may be frightened. By changing the patterns in your life, a transformation will take place. It may take a while to achieve, but every day will be a step nearer to changing your life for the better and getting you on the road towards more happiness. What you may find is that by un-winding and relaxing more, you will actually have more energy, which will then enable you to achieve more in less time!

Scary stuff sometimes. You may be in a position which although you don't like is, however, comfortable, a comfort zone that is familiar ground. Life could continue for as long as you like, just the way it is now, but you will just be going round and round in circles. To take the next step is a big decision but if you can you should give yourself a pat on the back and say to yourself "I want some changes to take place, I can do it, and I will do it however long it takes". It may be something really small in your life, or it may be a complete change, but whatever it is, only YOU know what it is and only YOU can change it. Don't be frightened, be positive. This is YOUR LIFE we are talking about, no one else's. You may have been living, in some ways, someone else's dream for example, or you may just be doing something which you have been doing all your life, so this can be a life changing experience but once you recognise that a pattern or situation has to stop, then take a look at how you can do it.

Activity

GET THE LIFE THAT YOU WANT

What I would like you to do is write down the changes that you would like to make.

Are these changes just within yourself or is someone else involved?
What are those changes?
How can you start to put them in place – what do you need to do?
How will you feel when things have changed?
How will it make your life different?

You may like to put on that list a few other things which may be holding you back

Start to make a list of the 'but's' in your life. Or should I change the word to 'if's' or 'if only' or 'because of'?
They are all really saying the same thing to you and by crossing them out of your vocabulary you will set yourself free from the chains of repetitive patterns in your life

A few examples –
Because my mother never praised me, I can never feel confident
But I was told at school that I was stupid, so I must be
If only my partner had not left me, how can I ever trust another person?
If only I had met you sooner
If only I had a better physique, I would feel more confident
If only this had not happened
I can't do this – I can't do that (no such word in the English dictionary)
These statements are excuses which you can let go of.

Turn some of those words around –
say to yourself – You can - .Don't say if – say When
Say - How can I.. not I can't.
Those few words create a whole different meaning

Changes may not happen overnight - so make an affirmation to yourself, that each new day is one step further on the road to where you want to be.

Whatever it is, and for each and every one of you it will be different, and the steps you take you have to feel comfortable with. This may be a whole new learning process or a little shift in yourself, but what you will be doing is moving on with your life and you can start to live it how you want. It will give you the opportunity to start enjoying your life, doing the things that you believe that you can, grabbing opportunities maybe that before you may have been afraid to take, and I can honestly say that much more laughter will come into your life. You will be enjoying it and you will feel much more confident, comfortable and relaxed, so the people around you will notice and may treat you differently.

What is it that you want to change? Is it something in you or the circumstances around you? Maybe you feel that you have too much to do and there are never enough hours in the day to do it all. Well perhaps by structuring your day differently, and prioritise what is important, it will free you. Whatever it is, you can do it. How you do it may be different for each and every one of you, but you are taking the first step, which is the most important. Once you recognise that your life could be better, and you could get more fun and contentment, you will start to realise that you will be much more at peace with yourself. That is such a beautiful feeling it is worth doing all that you can to reach it. You will know when you get there because life is not such a struggle. Life becomes what it is meant to be, beautiful and enjoyable and you will start to notice all the things that surround you. Once you start to believe in yourself, you will let your dreams start to become reality.

Now that you have the list in front of you, there maybe in there things that you think are impossible to change, but nothing is impossible. "How" I can hear some of you saying. Well, that is up to you. For each of you will have different circumstances, different ideals, different wants, and different ways to deal with things, but however you decide you want to change, then that is the right way to do it, as you have to feel comfortable and confident that things can get better, and you have to do it in a way that is right for you. It may be something very simple or it may be a life-changing situation, but whatever it is, take each step which feels right. There is no right way or wrong way, but just by wanting things to change, you are half way there. Putting it into practice may be another thing, but some of you may want to make a commitment to yourself that each day you will learn something that you can do to make this happen. Take each day as a separate day, and a day nearer your goal.

If there is something which you find yourself doing that you want to change, or someone around you is doing, then perhaps throughout the day, be aware of what you or they are actually doing and saying, be conscious of your actions, and perhaps at the end of each day, write down how you felt about things which have happened, and try and find perhaps a nicer way that things could have been done. Was it a negative day? Why? Was it a brilliant day? Why? What made it so brilliant or negative? Was it you or the people that you were with that made it so? Was it something that only happens occasionally or is it something that happens all the time? I think that when you start to understand **why** things happen, good and bad, then it enables you to look at your life realistically, and changes can start to be made.

Is it something quite major that needs to change? Is it your job, your relationships, your health? These types of changes can only take place if you deal with them. Look at changes that would be OK for you to put into place, maybe gradually, or by taking action now, like looking in your spare time for a new job, or asking yourself honestly why your health is poor? What really happened sometime ago that you can now put behind you? Wanting to improve things is a good start? But wanting and doing are completely different. How can you start to change habits of a lifetime? Some of you will not be ready to change something just yet, and this is OK. No one has to change if they are not ready, but as long as you know that the time *will* come, then that is all that matters. It will happen when you really want it to, and there is no way anyone can make you do it if you are not ready and willing. **The time has to be right.** You have to do it for YOU. No one else.

Changing things in your life is a major breakthrough. Sometimes just by changing the little things, then the bigger things change too. It is similar to when you throw a pebble in the pond, it has a ripple effect. Bigger things take longer obviously, but once you plant the seed to change, then things start to happen and new doors can open, life can be a lot more pleasant, and life can get happier. It will give you new freedom that you never thought you could have, because it frees YOU; yes you, as you begin to see life differently.

Probably the biggest thing for some people is that they need to realise that they need to change, or you may feel that if someone in your life changed, then your life would improve. But they will probably not be reading this book as they perhaps don't realise how they are affecting you, or they may do but do not know how to do things differently. Please, if you can, talk to them about it. Wow, that might be scary and frightening, or you may have done that in the past and it has not changed anything, but little by little things can change, and perhaps you need to change the circumstances of a situation for changes to happen. An example of this is how many battered wives put up with being hurt for so long, and then suddenly, from somewhere they get the courage and strength to move on with their lives. Suddenly something snaps, and it gives them the courage to do something about it. Very frightening and brave for them, but the relief and freedom it gives them comes very soon afterwards. It is the courage that is the hardest thing, and also the realisation that they don't need to go through all this torment. What have they done to deserve this? Probably nothing, but too many it is a way of life. They may have come from abusive parents so know no different, but until they recognise that, then they will continue to attract certain types of people into their lives and it is up to that person to change the pattern. No one else can break the pattern for them, again they have to do it themselves, and by changing the situation, it again opens new doors for them.

Thankfully, not all changes are as drastic as that. There are also the sorts of changes that give you more pleasure, satisfaction, enjoyment and can sometimes be a big step in a different way. You may be in a job you hate, are bored as hell, but you are frightened because of the security that the job gives you. You may be in a relationship that you no longer want to be in, or are frightened of being on your own so put up with things. Well really, if you want them to change, you can. Maybe not drastically, but even a little change would be better than nothing. I am not saying that you should walk out of your job or your relationship, but is there anyway that you can make it more enjoyable? Make the best of a bad situation by altering it to suit you. Take your time to think about it but honestly ask yourself what it is about your relationship or job that you don't like. At work, for example, perhaps if you had something else to do, or moved to a different department within the company - a new challenge can provide an amazing boost. It gives you motivation, it gives you a reason to look at your job differently, and maybe you could learn something new. Perhaps think about or even ask your boss if they would sponsor you if you went to college or night school to learn something that would help in your work, but would interest you at the same time, and you would be amazed at the age of the average college student. You don't have to be young to learn! Actually, lots of people start again with their education when they retire. It may have been something they had not had the time for earlier in life, and we are never too old to learn new skills.

A small shift in your thoughts could help make the day at work better. The workplace can be a challenging environment, but if you believe in yourself and appreciate your strengths, your skills and your abilities, but never sell yourself short, or bring yourself down, then others will value and appreciate you. You can step over obstacles if you recognise that they are opportunities presented to you so that you can rise to a new challenge, and if you do well, you will shine.

Try and make the most of the situation which you may have found yourself in, and change it to your advantage. Even small changes lead to bigger things.

Chapter 4
You are in control

*You will never be happier than you expect. To change your
happiness, change your expectations*
Bette Davis – 1908-1989

Thinking and feeling

Do you know that you can actually change your life
by changing the way in which you think? The Power
is Within You to do it. Our thoughts are what we make
them, and we can think positively or negatively about any
situation that we may find ourselves in. If we train our
minds to produce positive thoughts then we can achieve
what we want in life.

Only you can change the way you think and feel and
act, as you are the one with the Power. You are now in
charge of your own life, and you are also in charge of what
you get from life.

I am sure a lot of you have heard or read about positive
thinking, and some of you will feel that 'it's alright for people
to say that, but easier said than done' but I think if you
read on, you may come to your own realisation that there
may be some truth in it and it is easier than you think.

Our thoughts

I do not think any of us realise how powerful our thoughts can be. Everything that we think and do is part of our being. We have thousands of thoughts every single day, and some of the main thoughts we repeat to ourselves over and over again, until a clearer thought comes into our head.

But, if these thoughts are negative thoughts, then they will just go round and round in our head, and create more negative thoughts as sometimes our imaginations can run away with us. It is so hard when negative thoughts come, but we have a choice, we can overpower them. You can choose to continue thinking all the bad things, or you can change them. You can change them into positive thoughts, which bring actions. If you start to think positively about something, then this will spur you on to do something about it. Just try that for a minute, and see if I am not right. .

Through our thoughts, we can change our whole lives. If we want something, then we think about how that can be achieved, if there is something material that we need to go to the shop to buy, then we go don't we? If it is something more life changing, then we may take longer to think about it, but it can be done. Or, you can think on the negative side and say to yourself, "no I can't do that", or "I do not deserve that".

Just ask yourself one question. Why is it that some people move on with their lives and get more out of life than others? Is it that they are just lucky, or is it something that they are actually doing and thinking that has enabled them to move on? What I think you will find is that they THINK POSITIVELY about all life's situations and to them there is no other way to think. I think like that but occasionally I think negatively, but I then get cross with myself and without even thinking about it, I somehow change my thoughts as I do not like to feel down, and this is what negative thoughts do. Or sometimes something else I do is what I call 'faking it' to the outside world. If someone asks me how things are, I nearly always say wonderful, things are great even if they are not sometimes. I may know inside that things are not quite as good as they could be or have been, but to me they will be again soon, so I can not say to them or myself that things are negative because tomorrow or the next day things could and will be wonderful again. Even sometimes when I have been crying inside, I still 'mask' it to the outside world. My close friends may know different, but I have to think positively and it really works.

If you ask yourself whether in your general every day life you enjoy being down or miserable, or you like feeling sorry for yourself, telling everyone just how you are feeling then I am sure you will agree that the times in your life when things were going well were so much nicer. Just think about what your thoughts were like then. I think you will find that they were positive and it made you much happier. If we don't dwell on the negatives in life, then we can move on.

Sometimes when things happen in life that we are sad about, then it is OK to feel down, or miserable, and we have to work through these emotions. This is normal and part of the healing of the situation, so you should not feel bad about feeling negative at that time. Sometimes we can find ourselves in a negative situation which we have to work through, and I think we may all experience this sort of emotion at some time in our lives. Positive thoughts at this time can give hope and we often find that we learn something through these experiences, but we may not realise this at the time. It is often only when we look back after we have been through the experience that his becomes apparent. If we have days when we feel down and disheartened, then if we just accept that this is a 'blip' day and it will pass, then we should never feel guilty. It is something that we need to do, so if you can just accept it, acknowledge that is part of a healing process or just a bad day, then tomorrow can be different. It may be a couple of days that you need to 'withdraw' but that is OK. It will pass if you don't turn that 'blip' day into a downward spiral.

Our desires

Every thought and desire that we have, goes into our sub-conscious, and can be retrieved by us when the time is right. I will give you an example of this.

When my husband was doing well in his firm, he said that I could have a new car. I really do not like new cars and would have preferred a newer model of the car I had which was a very old BMW, but that would have been too expensive so I gave in and agreed to a car that I really was not that keen on, but it was new, so met his criteria. A few years later, after my divorce and my mother had died, I was in a position to change my car. Actually, in some ways I had forgotten about the red BMW, but it was in my sub-conscious. So, I decided to visit a friend who I trusted and had a car showroom. Well, guess what, on the forecourt and the first car that I saw was the exact car I had wanted years earlier, and was in my price range!

So, this was a thought that I had buried some years previously because the time for me to receive that car was not right then, as it gave me far more pleasure when I bought it myself. Actually I kept it for seven years!

What is it that you desire, and may have thought about either sometime ago, or more recently, that you would like to bring to fruition? My example was something materialistic, and your desires may not be the same, but if they are realistic, then why should you not have them? You will if they are right for you, when the time is right. (see chapter 7)

We cannot deny our feelings, and we cannot ignore them either

Emotions are something which are very hard to control, as we cannot always help how we feel, they are just there. You know sometimes when your heart beats a flutter, or your stomach may churn, these are emotions that just happen. You did nothing to make them happen, well you did actually, you may have bumped into the love of your life, you may have seen something that has frightened you, or something unexpected happened and it took you by surprise. When your heart actually flutters, this is something that you, yourself, cannot control. It is an expression of an emotion. Tears are another emotion that sometimes you cannot control. If something upsets you, tears can just flow, or you could see or hear something beautiful that reduces you to tears - they just appear.

Some people are more emotional than others. We are all different, but the feelings we experience are similar when they happen. I find it hard to understand how some people do not want to feel emotion. Is it that they have possibly cut off from their feelings, as a form of self-protection? I think maybe it is, but I find this sad. How can they love if they do not feel the emotion? Perhaps they think the pain will be too painful, as from past experiences they may have been hurt, but surely that does not mean that they will be hurt again. Sometimes they are, but maybe if they took more control in a situation, then they may prevent it happening again. Maybe if they had expressed their emotion at the time, and said how they really felt to someone, then maybe that person would not have hurt them. Expressing emotion can be hard sometimes, as often people do not want to hurt people's feelings, but sometimes it is better to be demonstrative than constrained. Withholding emotions can be self-destructive as your true feelings may come out later and be much more hurtful to that person. So many of us hide sometimes behind our true feelings and what is really happening.

If you can have 'honest conversations' with those close to you, it can be a good experience because you will begin to understand each other better. Sometimes we may hear something which we do not like, or we may say something which can be hard to say, but by bringing it out in the open, we actually dispel our fears and sometimes the not knowing is far harder. Our imagination can run away with us and get out of control. We can imagine all sorts of things, which really are not there. Maybe they are, but by confronting an issue, it becomes less of an issue. It can be hard as people don't want to hurt others sometimes, but you can be hurt far more with the not knowing. You may also be pleasantly surprised sometimes, as some people

139

find it hard to express how they feel, and maybe find it hard to show emotion.

Emotions and feelings go together really. There are obviously other types of feelings like pain. Physical pain and emotional pain are completely different, but physical pain can be just as hard to bear sometimes and can affect our emotions as sometimes they make us sad. To be in real pain possibly through illness, is a very emotional state and sometimes after an operation, quite dramatic. But, this is a time when usually you find yourself supported by friends and family. So why if you are in emotional pain say through a lost love, can you not share this with the same friends and family that may have been there for you in your physical pain? The time and the need are the same, but the emotion is different.

If you find yourself in emotional pain, why not try and express this and share it with those closest to you. A true friend or relation, who you also count as a friend, is invaluable.

So, how do we change our thoughts, emotions and feelings into a much more positive frame of mind? Good question, but I think you may have started to work that one out yourself, as I am sure that if you are feeling negative about something, then you may have started to realise that this does not have to stay that way, and you can change a situation to be much more pleasing to you which in turn will make you happier. "Wouldn't that be nice" I can hear some of you saying, but why shouldn't it happen? Just ask yourself that, and if you say well someone else has to change, then really you are just blaming him or her and not looking at the opportunity that is in front of you.

Your mind is not in control of you - you are in control of your own mind. Powerful thought but it is true. Only you know what goes on in your mind, and only you can change it. Yes, outside influences can have an enormous bearing on your thoughts, actions and feelings, but we actually are far more in control than we think. We can remove ourselves from a situation if we really want to, we can get that job that we really want to if we put our minds to it, and we can put to one side all the negative thoughts that we may have had in the past, and begin to think to ourselves that we deserve what is the best in life that we can have. Why shouldn't you have all that there is on offer, like fun, laughter, happiness, peace of mind and the joy of all the people that are in your life? We can achieve whatever it is that we want, but we have to work at it, we have to want to change things, and we have to look at ways that it can be achieved.

But the first way, is to think positively about any situation that you find yourself in, and look for the good things first. For example, you might not like your job, but there must be people you work with who you like, so is the situation really as bad as you think? If you find yourself surrounded by people who never see the good in you, surely they must have a good side, and you may have had many great times with each other, but sometimes the bad overtakes the good. Think of all the wonderful things you are surrounded with, your home, family, friends, the little things that you have in your possessions, and the memories that they may hold. Sometimes, and very often, we take for granted what we have, and do not give much thought to it, but if you stop and think how lucky you are, and start to appreciate what you have, then that is a step in the right direction. Really think about all the good that is in your life right now.

On the other side of the coin, if you do not have a job which I know can be hard for some, perhaps there are other things you can do like voluntary work which will give you a motive and a sense of purpose. Having a sense of purpose can give more meaning to your life.

If you want something really badly, then what is it that is stopping you doing what ever it is that you need to do to achieve your goals, or desires? Is it that you are not sure how to achieve something, and, if you didn't do this earlier, then why don't you write down all the necessary steps that you may have to take to achieve it, and then start to take one step at a time, to reach that goal, but never ever lose sight of it. Never give up if it is really something that you want. Why not make a plan on how you can reach your target, and perhaps set a time frame and at the end of that time, put a section in on how you will feel when you have achieved it? I bet that feeling will be something really wonderful.

If on the other hand you don't really know what it is that you want, and I know some people just drift in life, and have no direction, then perhaps it is time for you to sit down and really think what you would like to be doing in say three years time. Do you still want to be doing the same old thing, be in the same situation, or do you want to have something to work to, but you just don't know how or what? This sort of situation is not uncommon as there are a lot of people who do not know what it is that they want. Sometimes it will suddenly dawn on you later in life, as you are quite happy now. We do not all have big dreams, and often it is the people with the dreams who are the go getters and go out and achieve their dreams, and do whatever it takes as they have desire and passion. But, I think we can all have something that we can work to, or want perhaps later in life, so perhaps we will have to start to put thoughts and ideas into motion now. If we leave it, then our dreams never become reality. OK, the time may not be right now, but never lose sight of it and keep working at it, as nothing is given to those that sit back and do nothing. We have to work with it in our minds and thoughts, and sometimes actions, and then we can achieve it when the time is right.

But some things do take time to achieve, and often nothing will happen overnight, but it is the desire to get to the end of the rainbow that keeps you focused, and gets you what you want.

Do you realise that this could be a NEW BEGINNING for you. This could open up a whole new life for you, so don't be scared. This may be the start of a wonderful path - who knows where it will lead you, but it will be worth taking. Sometimes in life we do have to take chances if we want things to change, and if we believe that we will not fail, then we won't. OK, if we do fail at the first attempt, then try again, it will be worth it. I am sure a lot of you will find changes that are scary, and may not change everything at once, but just keep at it, day by day, week by week, and then suddenly you will start to feel alive, really alive, and it will be worth every step that you may have had to take, and it may happen sooner than you think. But, you do have to take action some times, change your way of thinking maybe, but this is your life we are talking about, no ones else's and I am sure that you want to get out of life all that you can, and for it to be as happy as it can be.

Following our feelings

If you let fate happen, and believe that it exists, then sometimes you might find yourself in the right place, at the right time, for you to achieve what it is that you want. You may just bump into the right person who can set you on the right path, or an idea may suddenly pop into your head with something that you would like to do, and it maybe a thought that you never realised was there. Or it may have been at the back of your mind for sometime and you have forgotten about it.

Have you ever had that feeling called 'gut instinct'? I am sure you have, when you 'just know' something is right, or, as the case may be, something is wrong. You could call it your intuition and it is much more powerful than many people realise. Well may be we should listen to our 'gut instincts' more often, and follow what it is telling us. Maybe you could call it 'a hunch' but when we have followed it, we know we were right to do so, so why don't we do it more often? There are loads of examples that have been reported over the years, when people say they just knew not to get on that train, to learn later that it had crashed, or someone has had an urge to make a certain phone call, and the person at the other end has needed them

There is also the other instinct that we have, when an idea pops into our head and we wonder where it has come from, but how often do we follow it through? Hopefully we do on most occasions, but I think if we 'listened' to ourselves, our thoughts and ideas, and start to understand that we actually do know what is best for us, then if we can start to 'trust' that we are going in the right, or wrong, direction and follow it through, then we often can make better choices

Your gut instinct, your intuition, your hunch, what ever you like to call it, is all part of your sub-conscious and your inner wisdom. It is like a wise person that has gone ahead

143

and seen the future and come back to tell us which way to go. It has seen the bigger picture of our life – the Grand Design you could call it, but it isn't always where we think we *should* be going. Sometimes we block it by putting up obstacles or thinking in our minds that we know best. But then when we do follow our inner wisdom we can then look back and realise that it was right to do so and sometimes it can be life changing. Sometimes if we are not sure which way to go, or what to do about a situation, then we should do nothing until we have a clearer thought or idea which you will then know is the right way.

Chapter 5
You are beautiful

When we find the beauty within, then we find the Secret.

Wow, wouldn't it be wonderful if we knew the Secret to a Life of Happiness? What a wonderful feeling it would be, and how peaceful we would feel. But how do we get there? How do we achieve it?

Some people have already learnt the secret and glow from inside, because once we learn to love ourselves for who we are, then the beauty inside can begin to shine. It doesn't really matter if you think you are good-looking or not. You won't see it in the bathroom mirror! Real beauty cannot be touched, or even seen with the physical eyes. You will see and touch true beauty when you feel your own inner peace. You will know and feel real beauty when you can give away anything with love and not want anything in return.

But this can be very difficult for some people. But once we begin to accept we are not perfect, we all do have faults, and looking back at our mistakes influences our lives more than we realise, then it is OK to say to ourselves that we are fine as we are and we can love ourselves for who we are.

All of us have beauty within but we do not always show it, recognise it, or accept it. Some of us do not even question who we are and those who do can find it a long and sometimes painful process. But once we find out who *we* are as a person, then we can start to feel at peace in the knowledge that we *are* beautiful. Once we do this it is amazing what begins to happen; we begin to radiate our inner beauty and our happiness shines through. This can be a very powerful experience.

You have the Power to have laughter, happiness and fun in your life and to be surrounded by love. Love for others, love for yourself, and love for what you have. Not what you want materialistically and for your comfort, but to really start appreciating what you have NOW and to enjoy it. Money cannot buy you happiness, it can help maybe, but there is so much more to life than money. Once you start to look around you and realise how lucky you are, you will start appreciating what you have. Also think about all the good things you have achieved and done. We all achieve so much but sometimes we do not realise it or forget. Perhaps it is time to start remembering and shouting to yourself and others about your good qualities, and the good things that have happened. Negative things can sometimes override the positive things in life, so just take a few minutes to remember all the wonderful things that have happened, how far you have come in your life, obstacles that you have overcome perhaps, and start to praise yourself. It will bring a smile, but don't put them to the back of your mind again. Keep remembering!

If you feel changes need to be made then you can make them happen and you will start to feel really alive again. You can make things happen if you really want to. Who knows what is around the corner for you, but isn't it worth finding out?

Nobody said life was going to be easy, but sometimes we have to follow our gut instincts in order to move on. Each step of our journey is a step further towards making our own lives more fulfilling and worthwhile, and to get all the pleasures and love in our lives that we can. Nobody I am sure wants to live a miserable life if they don't have to, but sometimes we may need to change things in our life so that we *can* be happier.

So why not make that change? Nobody deserves to suffer. What we have to do is work through some of the lessons we may have to learn. We all have lessons but first, we need to recognise what they are, then acknowledge them, then work through them; change a pattern that may have been running through our lives if necessary, and then we can begin to move on to a better life.

Some of us have bigger lessons to learn and go through life less easily than others, but by taking a good look at the life that we have, and the life that we would like, then we can start to create change. Yes, there probably will be mistakes along the way, but learn from them and forgive yourself and others and start to think positively about both. You may need to change your thinking, and thoughts, but it is worth it. (see chapter 4)

What we need to strive for is peace and harmony in our lives. Harmony is a lovely balance that we can achieve, both in work and relationships, and is so very important This, actually, is when you will have the freedom to move on and you will start to make choices that will create a better life and you will really like yourself for who you are, and appreciate all that you have.

Once you accept that the past is the past, and you are now ready to move on to the future, you can create a future that inspires you. Please, if you can, start to put any negative thoughts or habits that you may have behind you, forgive maybe yourself or others, and maybe stop feeling sorry for yourself, and start to live the life that is good. Look to the future with open eyes and really believe that things can change and they will.

Things may not change overnight, but you never know, miracles do and can happen, but the most important thing of all is that you want the best for yourself that you can, and as long as you strive for that, and believe that you can have it, then you will. But, it is only *you* that can make it happen, so why not make it happen? You can do it, you can have all the love in the world that you deserve, and the pleasures that come with it. Remember these little expressions

Love is what makes the world go round
The best things in life are free
Life is too short
Magic of Believing
So, let the past BE the past, and look to the NOW

Look around you and make the most of everything that you have NOW, and enjoy. Start by enjoying YOU. You may have to look deep within yourself to find the answers and it can be painful, but it is worth it.

If you feel things need to change then start to change them. If life is wonderful for you, and nothing needs to change in your life, then enjoy every moment.

They say 'a bride is never more beautiful than on her wedding day', which is the day that her beauty radiates, because of the happiness she feels inside. Be that bride.

Chapter 6
Believe in yourself

You cannot be lonely if you like the person you're alone with
Dr. Wayne W Dyer.

To believe in yourself is every person's right, and to love yourself is very important, because if you do not love yourself, then how can you expect others to love you. They will I am sure, but it is also important to remember that to love yourself comes from within. When you are happy with yourself, others will find you more complete. You will have self-confidence in all that you do; you will be more content and will accept life more as it is.

Believing in yourself is also about accepting yourself just as you are. When we can learn to accept and understand our good points as well as our bad points, we can begin to find out who we are as a person and have self-love. This is important because so often we never think about or question who we actually are. We are all individual people with our own identities, but some people find this hard as they feel they don't have a role. Others never question it and have the knowledge of their own identity since birth.

It isn't until we are older that we begin to realise how the influences in our childhood have shaped us into the person that we are today. If your parents believed in you and encouraged everything that you did, or wanted to do, right from childhood, then that is a brilliant place from which you can start to believe in yourself. Encouragement from

149

parents helps you develop into a person that is confident and independent. Praise is also important and I don't think we sometimes do enough of it. It can help with people's self esteem which is part of believing in oneself.

Some of you may have had a difficult childhood and your parents may have said little things which have had a big effect on how you may feel about yourself. For example, if your parents, in a rage often said "you're stupid, you can't do that, you are not good enough" etc then, said often enough, you will believe it. Some children are able to shrug these sorts of comments off and it does not bother them, but others can't. Often it is not meant in the way it sounds and parents do say things they regret when under stress, but continually putting children down will eventually mean they may grow up with all sorts of issues that they have to deal with in later life. Such thoughts put into your head in early life are very negative thoughts, and you may grow up always thinking that you are not 'good enough' or you 'cannot do better'. But hold on - you can because you deserve to feel good about yourself. If you can learn to overcome these 'hang-ups' then you will start to heal yourself. So, you may not have lived up to your parents expectations of you, you may have chosen a career which they did not approve of, they may have wanted you to follow their dreams, not yours. Saying No to them, you will do it your way, may be a very difficult thing for you to do, but this is your life, NOT theirs.

If it is a close family member that is putting you down, or controlling you, then maybe the time has come for you to talk to this person about it. They are holding you back and stopping you believing in yourself. It is time for you to move on. They may never change but you can. If we are doing what we enjoy then we are so much happier. If restrictions are put on you, for whatever reason, then you will feel suppressed and frustrated. Sometimes we have to take responsibility for ourselves and say that big word NO.

Every person is different, but I think we all want the same out of life - to love and be loved by all the people in our life right now, and to be able to do the things we want to, and to feel good about it. Sometimes it may be later in life, as you may have lost your confidence or in some way have been demoralised, so it leaves you with doubts. But these doubts can disappear as we learn to work through our issues one by one. Doubts are actually only thoughts and our fears, but all these things can affect you, and even if you don't realise it, sometimes in your sub-conscious there is a little nagging doubt. Somewhere along the way you may have got the idea that you could only exist if you did certain things to please others, or did it their way, not yours. But, you can overcome this by being you. Just you, as you are now. We all have fears or doubts in some form at some stage in our lives. Learning to overcome them is a powerful experience.

Believe in yourself that you are exactly where you are meant to be at this time in your life. No matter where you are in life, no matter what is happening, believe that you are doing the best that you can, and you will. By believing in yourself, it can really be up-lifting. Why not, why shouldn't you believe in yourself? It will get you wherever you want to be.

*You can only live it your own way and walk your own
journey
So don't feel guilty
Love yourself NOW- Start believing in you NOW
Start praising yourself NOW -
And don't look back*

You can, if you want to, achieve anything by believing you can and that you deserve it. I know this may be hard for some people but you are good enough, everyone is. Accept you may have had set backs, forgive the people who so demoralised you earlier in life, and believe in yourself. What you also have to learn to do is to like yourself. Like yourself for who you are, and learn to like others, and accept that we all have faults, and just put those negative thoughts about yourself and others to one side, and think of all the positive things about you and them. Positive thoughts are so much nicer, and there is good in everyone. Sometimes hard to see I agree, but there is, and by bringing the best out in yourself, and others, then you can start smiling again.

151

It will amaze you I am sure that when you start to believe in yourself, how you will feel. You will be more confident, you will be smiling, full of fun, and laughter will be an everyday thing. Laughter is one of the best tonics. You may even start to laugh at yourself, at some of the things that you have done over the years, and share it with friends who will see a different side to you and bring out the laughter. If you have a family, just see how they start to react to you. If they see that you are happy and more confident, then they will be happy for you.

Take a look around you, at people you know, and start by thinking of all the people in your life who believe in themselves, who are confident, always positive about things, and who like themselves. This is an important part, because if you start by liking yourself, then the rest can follow much more easily. I am sure if you ask your friends that believe in themselves, they will say that they also like themselves.

Believing in yourself will not happen over night. It can be a very difficult process for some people, but be patient. Take one step at a time, one issue at a time, and work through it either on your own or with the help of someone. A friend, partner or a professional if need be. It can be done and you really can believe in yourself, and like yourself. Other people do I am sure, so why shouldn't you? Often we find that as we get older we learn to love ourselves much more easily because we accept and know ourselves better. Getting to know and accepting the true person you are, is an important part of the process.

Activity

If it helps, a good way to do this is to do The Wheel of Life as it will show you where you are today. How happy you are with particular things, and what areas could be better? With the outside edge being happy, draw a line in each area as to how you feel about each. Spend sometime filling this in, don't rush it or draw your own version if you want. Then perhaps in 6 months time, take another look at it and see if one or two areas may warrant higher marks, and the changes that have happened.

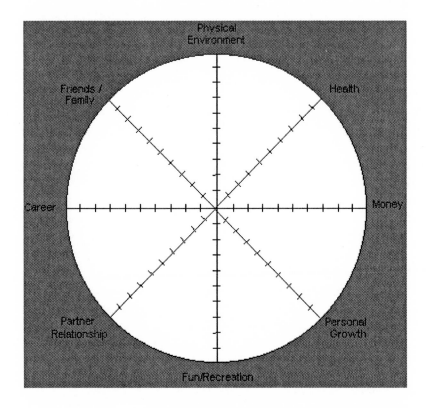

The Wheel of Life

Chapter 7
Be inspired...feel the passion

We act as though comfort and luxury were the chief requirements of life, when all that we need to make us really happy is something to be enthusiastic about

Charles Kingsley 1819-1875 English Author and Clergyman

If you do not have passion, inspiration will be difficult but if you find something that you truly believe in, then inspiration and the passion will follow. We do not all have big dreams or desires, as I did not myself a few years ago but when I did come across something that became my dream, I suddenly felt so different.

When you have passion all sorts of emotions and feelings emerge. You can begin to feel 'alive' because you have a buzz running through your whole body which makes you so passionate about what you want to do, and you just run high on the energy that you get. It creates excitement, and you have this nervousness about you because your mind is so excited about what you want to do. Your mind may not sit still! Write all your ideas down as you get them, as sometimes you will not remember them, as they can flash through your mind at very inconvenient moments. Keep a book with you at all times including by your bed. Or if you prefer, have a tape recorder with you so you can speak into it with your thoughts.

Sometimes you have to ignore the 'parrot' that may be sitting on your shoulder trying to block your inspiration by saying "no" to the if's and but's that it talks to you about. They just disappear if you are really determined. You can then turn those words into 'I can' and 'I will'. A good example of this is this book.

When I first started writing it, it really was just for my children and grandchildren but the words just flowed and a letter evolved into a book! I became so passionate about it. What I began to realise was that I wanted to share all my experiences and some of the knowledge that I had gained over the years. We all have so much knowledge that could be shared with the younger generation but it seems that we still have to learn from our own mistakes because the life skills learnt by our parents and forefathers are lost in the gaping hole we call the 'generation gap'.

I had to work out in my mind how I was going to share my experiences. But I knew that I could, and I now realise the importance of writing the book because it is allowing me to move on with my life.

When I decided that this was the right way forward because I believed in it so much, what I started to do was visualisation. I visualised myself having a copy of my book in my hands. I visualised myself standing up in front of some people talking about it, signing copies, laughing and joking with them and it worked. I had no idea how successful it would be, but that did not matter. Because of my belief, it became my passion and consumed me. But I enjoyed it. The parrot spoke to me many times during the final stages of the editing and I had quite a few sleepless nights. But my belief and I suppose you could call it 'my drive' was still there, so I overcame them. Visualisation is a very powerful tool which can be applied to any situation. I did actually used to think that it was silly and would never work, but I now realise how powerful it can be. You can visualise yourself in any situation that you want, but what you need to do is say to yourself that you have it 'now' Don't wish it, think well maybe, because your sub-conscious will get confused. Act as though it has happened and it will.

What you also have to do is 'think big'. If you aim for the top or success then you will reach it. No-one actually starts

155

at the top, you have to make your own way there, step by step, little by little, but never loose sight of where you want to be. Keep focused and yes there will be a time when the going gets tough, but keep at it and you will achieve. Don't give up. So many entrepreneurs failed at sometime, came across obstacles, challenges and disappointment but one thing they all did was never give up and learnt from their mistakes, and tried again. A classic example is Thomas Edison who was reportedly asked; Why do you keep trying to create an electric light when you have already failed 10,000 times? He is said to have answered that he had not failed 10,000 times but rather that he had successfully discovered 10,000 ways that it didn't work, and each discovery he became closer to finding the one breakthrough that would succeed and of course the rest is history. So persistence is trying to find the right way around an obstacle if things go wrong

We all have different dreams, ambitions, wants and desires and some of you may have a passion that you have had for a long time and never done anything about it. Why not start to look at ways that can help you realise your dream? Scary stuff, as it might mean taking a big chance and lead you into unknown territory. But do you want that passion to remain a dream? Why not make it reality? Think how it will enrich your life, but you have to take the first step, and then it will all fall into place. Yes you will have to work at it, sometimes working harder than you ever have, but because you will be enjoying it (well most of it) it is so rewarding and up-lifting. It brings a true sense of purpose to your life, and it will make you feel more fulfilled. Excitement gives you energy you never thought you had! It could be anything that you like, and only you know what it is. It can re-motivate you and give you another reason to reach your goal. Sometimes we can become complacent and this can give us the 'kick up the backside' that we need! Not every one has a dream or passion that they want to pursue, and that is OK as well.

Start by believing in these three little words 'Magic of believing'. Once you can do that your belief will turn into magic. Say these three little words to yourself over and over again and they really will bring magic into your life.

The word 'magic' on it's own has a different meaning but strung together with others, creates and becomes magical or magnetic which you will also become because you will have created your own magic! Your face will suddenly light up as the beauty of your inspiration shines through and smiles appear. You will start to draw positive things to you, your thoughts will become positive, and you will run high on the satisfaction and energy you will get.

A chance is nearly always worth taking and in some ways what is life without a challenge? Ask yourself how you will feel at the end of your life, if you have not pursued what you wanted to do. Do you always want it to be 'if only'?

Activity

If your dreams or desires were not included in an earlier activity
Then write them on a piece of paper.
They can be something quite small or major
Make a list of the things you need to put into place for this to happen.
Where do you see yourself in 3-5 years time?
What would you like to be doing and with whom?
Ask yourself if this would be just your dream or does it include anyone else?
What would it entail financially and could you achieve this?
Write down a timescale that would be possible to realise your dream.
Ask yourself if this is just a wish or could you do it?
If it is not just a wish, then ask yourself what is stopping you?

And lastly on that piece of paper – write how you would feel WHEN you achieve it. Not if, but when!
Then stick the piece of paper in a prominent position so you can see it every day – so your dream or desire does not disappear.

Chapter 8
You and your friends

A true friend knows your weaknesses,
but shows you your strength,
Feels your fears, but fortifies your faith,
Sees your anxieties, but frees your spirit,
Recognises your disabilities, but emphasises your possibilities.

William Arthur Ward – Educator

When I started writing this book, it came about because I realised that I did not know much about my parents and I did not want my children or grandchildren not to know who I am. I have had some extraordinary experiences which they will only learn about in *My Letter– the first part of this book*. These experiences have made me the person that I am. All of us have had experiences that other people may not know about and that you may always want to keep secret. But I think it is important for people to start thinking about who you are, and who your friends and family are. By getting to know them, they will get to know you better, and it may help people to be more understanding, and interested in you as a person, rather than saying "Oh that is just so and so" and never ever thinking more deeply about you. Hopefully, most of your relationships will be wonderful just as they are, but some relationships that you may have, may need to be changed for you to enjoy each other more.

I like to think that relationships come in two forms; friends and family. There are different levels of friends. True and special friends; close friends; friends; and acquaintances. Hopefully, all of us will have a variety of friends in our lives, and as anyone with a good, true friend will know, you will probably understand quite a lot about that person as you will have been through lots of good times, and bad, and will always have been there for each other. Oh, how precious they are and aren't we lucky to have them in our lives. Sometimes I think what would I do without them? I feel I am very lucky and have a lot of good, true friends, and I appreciate every single one of them as they are an important part of my life. Other people will be just as happy with one or two close friends as we are all different. I know this may seem a strange thing to say, but you do have to work at friendships. Friendship is a two way relationship. Whether it's a friendship between you and a man or you and a woman, it will need to be cherished and 'looked after' so always take care that you do.

True friendship in any form can take a very long time to establish, but it is so nice when you really know each other well. Some of my friendships I have had since I was a teenager and we are still friends now, friendships that have lasted for nearly 40 years. Other friends I have met over the years, either at work or socially, have become extremely close. Strangely enough, when I think about it, we are all similar types of people but we actually all come from entirely different backgrounds. To know who *you* are, look at the friends around you as energy always attracts.

One thing we all do is respect each other and we seem to accept each other for who we are. Every relationship should be like that but is not always the case. I think once we get to know and understand each other it is easier to accept people just as they are. Understanding someone can make a huge difference in a relationship.

Some people prefer not to have any close friends, only acquaintances, and some people like it that way. Everyone is different and some people are very private. Others do not know *how* to have a friend, and push people away sometimes without realising what they are doing. Often they maybe grumpy miserable people and it is their choice, or sometimes and very often just too shy, or have low self-esteem. If you know someone like that, why not give them another go at being their friend. Think how lonely they are. It may be their choice I agree, and they may not want anyone else in their lives, but maybe and I say maybe, underneath they do. I am sure the shy and low-esteem people would benefit enormously and will be brought out of their shells, and think how rewarding that would be, to them and you. It is hard for some people, but some people really are worth getting to know, and it would be so nice to have helped that person blossom, and grow in some way. You may find it easy to make friends, as I do, but we are not all like that.

Friendships mean different things to different people. You don't have to have a close friend in your life if you don't want to, but the friends that you do have, cherish them, they are in your life because they want to be.

If you have friends in your life who are always negative about things, or who are not supportive of you, then let them go. You don't need people in your life like that. They can pull you down and drain your energy and basically, feed off you. It may be painful to part, but concentrate on your other friends and develop perhaps a closer relationship with them. Positive people can be so much more uplifting and fun to be around. A lot of people have realised that sometimes not all of their friendships are good for them, and when they turn to their friends, sometimes in a time of real need, they find out just who their true friends are. Sometimes that true friend is a surprise to you, and a friend that you thought would be there isn't, but I think generally if someone in your life never sees any good in you, then they are not worth having in your life. A good, close friend may not be able to support you at a particular time, but they are just as important being there in the background. Each friendship will be different, but anyone in your life who never sees the good in you, or who never returns the friendship in the same way that you do, then really do you need them in your life? We all should celebrate the good things in our lives and try and move on from the negative areas. Friends should be encouraging you, not demoralising you. If you don't know how to let that person go, without hurting them, then just gently ease off the friendship. Perhaps stop phoning so often, make excuses why you can't meet, or just spend less time with them, and I think you will find that in time you will just drift apart and new people will start to come into your life, and theirs, and they will be just the people you need for you to move on in your life.

Simple Friends V Real Friends

A simple friend has never seen you cry
A real friend has shoulders soggy from your tears

A simple friend thinks the friendship is over when you
have an argument
A real friend knows that it's not a friendship until after
you've had a fight

A simple friend hates it when you call after he/she has
gone to bed
A real friend asks why you took so long to call

A simple friend, when visiting, acts like a guest
A real friend opens your refrigerator and helps him/herself

A simple friend wonders about your romantic history
A real friend could blackmail you with it

A simple friend expects you to always be there for them
A real friend expects to always be there for you!

Anon

The friends that are in your life are there because they want to be. You will each value the friendship I hope. But do you really know and understand them as well as you think you do? When you really listen to what they say, do you really HEAR? Do you accept them just as they are? I hope so, because no one on this earth is perfect and we all have faults, but we all also have more good in us than we realise. Understanding someone can make a huge difference in a relationship. If you really begin to LISTEN, you will be amazed at how much you will learn about your friends, and be surprised at the strength of the bond you create between you. Listening is quite a skill actually. Just try this on some of your friends, or family and see how many people get it right

---

Activity

Get your friends to imagine a car journey and they are the driver of the car. Just say "you are driving a car along a road, and the car turns a corner. Then the car continues along the road until it has to turn another corner, and another, then the car goes past a duck pond at the side of the road and so on until the driver turns another corner and comes to the end of the journey". Then ask everyone how old is the driver?

Well, you will be amazed at how many people didn't listen very closely at the beginning because they were more interested in what was coming next. But if they had listened they would know the age - because it is their own age. If you are addressing a group of friends, please say "if you know, please don't shout out your answer yet" and just watch the group's reaction. It will be quite interesting.

"Silent and listen are spelled with the same letters!"

By listening to friends and family, it shows not only that you really care, but that you believe in them. How important that can be, and isn't it nice to know that they believe in you too. But you may have not looked at it like that, and just accepted their friendships, but it can help with people's self- esteem, and often it may help you to begin to understand each other more. Just think about the time that you met, and how you jelled, and how the relationship has moved on over the years. But, was there a reason that you met, did that person bring something into your life that may have been lacking, or was that person just there? Often you can meet new people because you have moved on in your life in some way, and they have common interests which you can share, but what did that person do in their life before they met you, what sort of life did they have? Maybe very similar to your own, or completely different, but you are friends now, so enjoy them and really get to know them if you can. With friendships that have been established for a long time, you will know quite a lot about that person as you will have talked over the years, or have you? Friendships, like relationships, can grow much more if you let them have wings. Smothering them, being jealous of them or controlling is not healthy in any relationship, but does happen sometimes. If only people realised how damaging to themselves this is, because they not only hurt others, but they are stopping themselves from moving on as well.

By letting that friendship have wings, you let yourself and them develop into a much more fulfilled person, and you will both get much more out of the relationship than you may, at first, realised. You not only help yourself, but you help them too. You are not trying to lead their life for them, you are part of it, but everyone has their own journey that they are going on and you are a part of that. Part of that friendship, whether with a friend or family member, is to be compassionate and to enjoy sharing the moments that give you happiness together so that you see the beauty of life through the bond you develop with one another and what a wonderful gift that is to share between you. It is also about supporting each other in their time of need, but never be judgemental.

Activities to help you listen and hear

*Why don't you start and REALLY get to know the people in your life NOW. Whether it is a friend, or a family member that you don't KNOW properly. Perhaps, if you could start to ask questions about something that you may find interesting about them, this may lead to other questions being asked. You may also want to share some of your experiences with that person, so that **they** can get to know **you** better too, which is just as important.*
Write a list of the people who are important to you and a question by each of them, and make a column for yourself.

*What I would like you to do is **really listen** and **hear** what that person says. Just listening is quite easy, but really **hearing** what that person says is so important and you will learn so much more. By hearing, you remember.*
It will also help you understand that person better

Please also respect someone's wishes if they would find it too painful to share something, and they say no. Perhaps by you just showing an interest, it may enable that person to talk about it at another time, but it may not be to you. It may help to heal that person within, but please do respect them if they say no.

I hope that you can find the time to do this, and not put if off as 'you are too busy' or 'it is not the right time'
Take your time writing the questions, because each one is important.

Take some time to actually listen to others speaking and listen to the words that they use. Some people never use negative words or actions; others use them all the time. Listen to the way the words are said, and watch the expressions on the person's face who is saying it. Then think about what message they are sending out by their words. Positive words obviously bring action but they will also bring an enthusiasm to that person. Negative or depressing words work in the opposite spectrum so try and be conscious of the words that you speak because you will also be sending out your own message which you may not have realised at the time. Sometimes we really are not aware of what we are actually saying – we don't think about it enough unless it is an important speech. Make all your speeches important and your message will get across much better. (see also chapter 9)

This is something I came across a little while ago which is long but I think says such a lot:

Too busy for a friend – never

One day a teacher asked her students to list the names of the other students in the room on two sheets of paper, leaving a space between each name.

Then she told them to think of the nicest thing they could say about each of their classmates and write it down. It took the remainder of the class period to finish the assignment, and as the students left, each handed in their papers.

That Saturday, the teacher wrote down the name of each student on a separate sheet of paper, and listed what everyone else had said about that individual.

On Monday, she gave each student his or her list. Before long the entire class was smiling. "Really" she heard whispered "I never knew that I meant anything to anyone" were some comments. No one ever mentioned those papers again. She never knew if they were ever discussed, but it didn't matter. The exercise was done. The students were happy.

Several years later, one of the students was killed and his teacher attended the funeral of that special student. The church was packed with his friends.

As she stood there, one of his friends came up to her "Were you Mark's teacher?" he asked. She nodded "yes." "Mark talked about you a lot." Mark's mother and father were there and wanted to speak to her. "We want to show you something" his father said taking a wallet out of his pocket. "They found this on Mark when he was killed. We thought you might recognise it".

Opening the wallet, he carefully removed two worn pieces of notebook paper that had obviously been taped, folded and refolded many times. The teacher knew without looking, that the papers were the ones on which she had listed all the good things each of his classmates had said about him. "Thank you so much for doing that" his mother said. "As you can see, Mark treasured it". Then all Marks classmates started to gather around. All smiling but rather sheepish and they all one by one said they all had their own lists and what they meant to them all.

That's when the teacher finally sat down and cried. She cried for Mark and for all his friends who would never see him again.

Chapter 9
You and your body language

The body says what words cannot
Martha Graham 1893-1971

Has someone complimented you recently on something you may have done or how you looked? How did you react? Did you say, "thank you," and mean it, or did you make excuses or, perhaps, even laugh and turn away, or blush as it may have made you feel uncomfortable. Your body language will have revealed all!

Some people seem unable to receive compliments in the way that they should be received. A compliment is given to you for a reason, and because the person saying it really means it, so there is no reason to feel uncomfortable.

If you do not believe me, just try it on your work colleagues, friends and family. See who receives it in the spirit it is given, and see who feels uncomfortable. I remember doing this exercise at college while on my counselling course, and I was astonished at the reactions of the people who I thought were very confident.

We all deserve compliments and should know that the person giving the compliment is doing so because they want to, so the next time someone gives you a compliment, just stop and think before you do, or say, anything. Just stand still, smile and say, "thank you, how nice of you to say so". This actually is very hard for some people to do, but please just try it. I think afterwards you may feel very good about yourself, and so you should.

Also, can you start to give more compliments to your friends and family? It will help them to start to feel more confident, it will bring a smile to their face. And, in return, you will get pleasure from their smile.

But, how do you give a compliment to someone who may have his or her arms crossed so you get the feeling that nobody is allowed passed this "barrier" that they have put up. What is that person saying to the people around him or her? I am sure they do not realise the signal they are implying by crossing their arms. It can be a form of protection the person needs to display, as they may feel uncomfortable about themselves or the situation. It is not unusual behaviour to cross your arms, but if we can try and feel more relaxed and less stressed or apprehensive about things, then we will feel more at ease. If you find yourself doing this, try and practise standing with your arms by your side, or maybe hold something in your hands, and be aware of actually how you are feeling, and why. Then perhaps question why you felt like that, and what you can do to change that feeling.

Body language is actually quite interesting, and can be fun to practise and watch. It is also very important, as first impressions are so crucial. Within a couple of seconds or minutes the other person will make an instant judgment about you. So if you can smile, relax and appear friendly then you will create an instant bond with that person.

Just look at couples that are in love, and you will see that they face each other all the time, they may touch each other often, smile and actually look into each others eyes, and lean forward towards each other. If we feel comfortable with ourselves, then often you will find yourself facing the person that you are talking to, maybe you will lean towards them if you are really interested in what they are saying, and sometimes with friends, we actually touch each other more than we realise. Or do we? Some people feel very uncomfortable if touched, say on the arm, but it can be a little gesture which says a lot. Someone who is feeling comfortable and open, you will find puts their hands behind their head, or sits in a fashion that you can approach them easily, which is so much nicer. Once we become aware of body language, just watch and observe others. It really is quite interesting and can be very amusing. I could go on about this subject in lots of ways, like they say if people look down or to the left, or rub their nose when they are talking to you, they are telling a lie, but why I am mentioning this briefly, is for you to be more aware of other people's body language and your own, so that you are perceived in a more relaxed way.

Body language is also about how we feel about our bodies, and so many people feel uncomfortable with how they look that they may hide behind clothes, as the media has given the impression that you have to be stick thin to look good. That statement is not true. So many people who do feel comfortable with themselves, whatever their size, stand straight, hold themselves well, and ooze confidence with their style, not just in their clothes but within their manner.

Hopefully, we can all start to realise that our size does not matter, but our appearance does, and if we try to dress in clothes that we feel comfortable in, look smart and clean, make-up on if necessary, then we can go outside and say to the world, I am ME, this is who I am, and I like me for who I am. I think this little saying that I came across a while ago says it all

I have learned that we are all the same......
only the details are different!

Anon

Chapter 10
You as a parent

Age does not protect you from love, but love to some extent
protects you from age
- Jeanne Moreau

We are becoming much more aware these days of the subject of bringing up children. Seeing television programmes on the subject and watching psychologists going into homes with a camera we are all learning a great deal with ideas on how best to be a parent whatever our social status. It is not always easy and I am sure a lot of us would love to wave a magic wand and our children will suddenly become perfect. Unfortunately it is not that easy but we certainly can learn from these programmes and I certainly have revisited moments which taught me a great deal. I would like to share with you some ideas and suggestions which you may be able to relate to.

The world is becoming a multi cultural society and of course we all have our own morals and disciplines we inherit from our own parents and our own cultures, but it is an important role being a parent, I am not sure whether we realise just how important. We are our children's teachers and the examples that we set, will leave an impression on our children for the rest of their lives. This is an enormous responsibility, and quite scary if we actually sit down and think about it. Bringing up our children can give us so much pleasure, we can be really proud of them now and in later life. But it is not always easy.

Our children are a reflection of ourselves as we are a reflection of our parents. That's how the next generation grows. We make choices that we believe to be right at the time, but in some ways, there is no right or wrong way. We learn from our children as they learn from us and we grow together. As parents we learn how to raise children from how our parents reared and taught us. They were our role models, and they learnt from their parents. Patterns are formed through generations, therefore, the only "lessons" we are given in parenting (apart from reading up on the subject) are inherited and come down the line from generation to generation, even then we only take on board what we feel is right. Society is changing all the time and often we feel we need to change 'with the times' as some of our values may be different or out dated.

Sometimes we judge, we do not agree with something that our parents may have done, the way in which it was done or an example that they have set us. We may decide that is not the way we want our children to be brought up and it is every parent's right to do so, as we can only do what we feel comfortable with.

So we, as parents, are there for our children to guide and teach them as they grow. Each child will have a different personality, ability, or physical attributes. Some of these are inherited and are part of their genetic make-up and together with their own personality makes them individual people. What a lot of parents may not realise is that each of our children are on their OWN JOURNEY and we cannot live their life for them. It is every parents wish to want the best for them, to protect them from harm. Hard as that may be to realise, we really are just here to guide them and be their support and we have to try and do it in a way that is right for them and us. We may see things differently because their generation (and ours) often have different values, and see things in a different light. We should not forget that children also teach us things throughout their lives.

Sometimes it is really hard to stand back and watch our children making mistakes or failing. There is a very fine line between when the time is right to step in and when the time is right to take a back seat. None of us wants our children to get into trouble, but sometimes our children have to learn their own lessons, we maybe hindering the process if we keep helping "to pick them up" when mistakes are made; this is where guidance comes in. One thing that we shouldn't do is try to control them through threatening them. Children will and do make mistakes as they grow, that is part of life, and that is how they learn. (That is how we learnt.) A child may become frightened if punished for every little mistake he or she makes, how can they learn the degree of their mistake if whatever they do is punished for? This will only create fear and the least mistake might prevent them from being adventurous and taking chances. We often learn more from our mistakes, so why shouldn't they?

There is also the other spectrum when we are sometimes too lenient with them and set no ground rules down or guidelines. Children benefit from structure and have to learn boundaries and they need to know what they are. Children will actually respect you more, even though they may not agree with some of them as they get older. Each child is different so if we can talk to our children and explain how we may feel, and why we have a set of standards then hopefully they will understand if all their wishes are not granted!

We also need to have our own ways of disciplining our children because each child may respond differently to their siblings. What works for one may not necessarily work for another, but what we must always do is follow through with the discipline that is imposed, they will then learn not to cross those boundaries. Often it is easy sometimes to let things slip and not follow through but this can confuse the child, and referring back to the television programmes we can see that sticking to the rules really does work.

Sometimes if things go wrong for our children, we blame ourselves thinking that we may not have been good parents, and some people feel guilty and feel they have failed in some way. There comes a point when we have to begin to hand the responsibility over to them so that they can start to make their own way in life. Sometimes outside influences lead children to rebel and may even take them on a downward spiral towards being out of control. As long as they know and feel loved at home, and they can return to us in time of need, it's then that we know we have played our part.

Children themselves have to learn about life, and what a challenge it is. It is a big, big world out there and they need to learn how to cope and should be able to feel confident about themselves, so that they can face the challenges they meet

But how do we make a child feel confident enough to cope? How do we encourage our children to stand up for themselves? How do we encourage a child to be top of the class? They can't all be top so the most important thing we can give our children is a feeling of self-esteem that comes from giving them love and being happy. No matter how bad they may be sometimes, or if they are unsuccessful at something, they need to know that their parents love them, and will encourage them and support them in everything they do; it will help them grow into confident adults. As confident people they can then learn to take chances in life and will not be afraid to do so, they have the knowledge that it is OK for them to live their own dream, and become the person that they want to be. Yes, they may make mistakes along the way, but confident people find it so much easier to pick them selves up and start again. Every child is special and has special qualities, these should be developed along with the help of parent's encouragement so they can shine, be happy and confident so they will feel good about themselves.

Sometimes, parents can push their children too hard, and put pressure on them. Yes, some children thrive on pressure and need just that little push and encouragement, but a little push and a big push are very different and too much can sometimes lead to stress. We all want to see our children do the best that they can in all areas of their lives, but mainly it is more important for the child to be happy - then they will do their best. If a child, for whatever reason, is unhappy, then how can that child enjoy life's challenges? An unhappy child loses confidence, loses their self-esteem, and the downward spiral begins. It is then very hard to bring that child up to like who he or she is; to find the positive aspects of the circumstances that they find themselves in, and to have the confidence that they will succeed. So maybe they start to get into trouble or give up and don't work as hard as they should. Sometimes this is a cry for help and often they don't know how to deal with things or know whom to turn to because they may feel that they have not lived up to our expectations. Children these days are surrounded by peer pressure from outside the home in their schools and colleges and from their friends so it is hard for them to compete sometimes.

It may be useful and interesting to ask our own parents about how they were raised as children. Some parents refer back to their own experiences all the time and often compare, others never talk about their life, but it may help to explain certain things. They were raised in a different generation to us, so possibly their values were different, but what was their childhood like? How were they themselves disciplined by their parents? How were they punished if they did something wrong? Were rules set down and what were they? Did they break them or abide by them? Did they suffer from peer pressure? Did they follow their own chosen career path or did they feel that they were influenced by their own parents? The list of questions you may want to ask can vary but it could help you understand your own parents better.

So parents are learning all the time and I think this should sometimes be explained to our children. We are learning as well as them, we do not have a reference book to refer to each time something happens and if things do go wrong, then we should all try within the family to work through a situation, and not blame each other. Children blaming parents and parents blaming children can often become a vicious circle. When things go well, we should all congratulate ourselves as having both done a good job and praise each other. Praise is such a powerful boost to anyone's self-esteem. Perhaps we should praise each other more often, even over the little things they do or achieve and not leave it to just the big achievements. Perhaps we should make as much as we can of birthdays, this is a great opportunity to celebrate a child's special day, and an opportunity to let them know how much we care.

But to make children happy some parents feel that buying all the presents the children want, and spending all you're hard earned money on them is the answer, but is it? Do you think that **all** the presents will be remembered in years to come? If you look back over your own life, you will have remembered a few presents; the presents that really meant something to you. What children do remember are the little things. The time you spent together, the special moments that you shared, the outings perhaps which were special. Those memories are far more important than just spending money on them. Those presents will not make them happy forever. Maybe it will in the moment, but not long term. But peer pressure is difficult to overcome and the day WE ALL realise that material things are not what matters, is the day we all become happier.

Perhaps we have to ask ourselves if this is right and why some of us buy everything instead of spending quality time with each other and talking. Children of course have different interests but some children are loosing their social skills because they spend so much time on their own as it may be easier or necessary for the parents. Often they spend hours playing games or watching television and if un-supervised these are often violent, and children then believe this is a normal way to behave. How is he/she going to learn social skills that will be needed in later life?

The days of playing in the street maybe gone, but there are others ways for children to interact. Our next generation need to learn how to cope in the big wide world when they are older and facing their own challenges. It is an exciting time for them and they need to learn how to be competitive, interact with others, be social and have respect. Fortunately most children do learn these skills but sometimes for some, not until later in life.

We seem to be bringing up our children in a world which has gone crazy! Crazy for material possessions instead of simple pleasures that life has to offer. The police believe that the word 'respect' has left many children's vocabulary and I understand many other people in authority agree with them. The child's excuse is often that they are bored, and therefore get themselves into trouble because there is nothing else for them to do. Actually children of this generation have more material things than any other generation but all too often don't know how to interact as they may have become isolated from their peers.

Children who are encouraged to have a hobby, play sports, read or socialise during their free time are much more likely to grow up as a team player, more confident and are often more ambitious as the confidence that they have gained has helped them feel good about themselves. Sometimes it can be hard to encourage a teenager to do some thing else other than sleep all day or take part in a hobby, but if he or she is encouraged right from an early age, then children seem to grow up with more enthusiasm to enjoy their free time. As they grow older hormones of course come into play and can be such a difficult time for them, (and us) but as long as we know that this stage will pass, and it does, then the frustration that it can cause has to be recognised and the less pressure we put on them, the more good we do. Encouragement and praise is more important than getting frustrated but that can be very difficult in some situations. We must also try not to put everything down to hormones and make it an excuse. The most important thing we can do is keep the relationship alive and hopefully on an even keel. Praising them really does work so much better than shouting at them. Difficult to do sometimes because it is so hard when they shout back! Unfortunately all too often they are mirroring us, the examples we may have set them without realising what we were doing. We can't be perfect all the time and neither can they! Perhaps this needs to be explained which may help in the difficult times.

Only you as a parent know what sort of relationship you have with your own child, and that relationship has to be continually worked at and not just taken for granted. It is like a husband and wife relationship and friendships, they all have to be worked at, and so we have to work with our children, not against them.

Whilst writing this chapter these thoughts came to me.

We can admire our children and tell them how much we
love them and how clever they are.
We can tell them how proud we are of them.
We can encourage them to discuss and share their
feelings.
We can encourage our children by supporting them in a
positive way.
We can praise our children, but also point out that they
learn from their own mistakes.
We should encourage them to be honest with themselves
and truthful to others.
We can encourage them not to feel a failure if they are
not top in everything they do, by pointing out other
qualities they possess.
We can help our children to develop respect for
themselves, and others.
We should never demoralise our children.
We should help them build on their self-esteem

Sometimes parents are too busy to spend time with their children. Sometimes work takes priority, and it may be very necessary for you to go to work, either for the extra money or your own sanity, and they may be cared for while you are at work, or you may be working hard at home looking after the family. But sometimes that child, without telling you, feels neglected and pushed to one side. Most children cope well with being cared for by other people than their parents, but sometimes the stresses from everyday living can take over when you are working, so that, maybe, when your child wanted to tell you something or wanted to share their day, they may have felt that you were unapproachable or it was inappropriate at that moment. A child may then start to bottle up his or her feelings, and when you do spend quality time together, other things take over and it has been forgotten or put to the back of their minds, and they do not want to bother you. This then can build up to be quite a burden for that child and they will not know how to deal with it. They may not have realised that they could have shared their problems, as and when they occurred, because they may have felt that your life was too busy so you couldn't spare a moment. This is where failure to communicate and recognising other people's needs may begin to develop. Sometimes it takes more than a moment to listen to them. But however long the moment is, it is always a precious moment.

One thing we do need to mention to our children is that parents also need their own space sometimes, and we should not feel guilty about taking time off from them. It is important, to have quality time on your own, to do your own thing, as you still have your own lives to lead. Yes, they are a part of it but by not being on top of one another all of the time we can lessen the stress that sometimes happens between parents and children and the relationship can deepen as a result. So, do try and take some quality time for yourself and not feel guilty about it.

Parenthood is a very difficult responsibility that we take on, and I am sure when you first learn that you are about to become a parent, you have no idea what actually lies ahead. If you did, then some of you may think again, as it can be a daunting experience, but I am sure most of you feel that children, however good or bad they are, are worth all the time and effort that you put in. They also teach us many things and can bring an enormous amount of joy. Even if you become estranged from your child along the way, for whatever reason, somehow you will find you have unconditional love for them. Surely this is what parenthood is all about.

Chapter 11
You can fail...it's OK

We can do no great things, only small things with great love
Mother Theresa

Have you ever given yourself permission to fail?
I have noticed that some people are so hard on themselves and self-critical if they do not "make the grade". Whose grade - theirs or someone else's? By whose standards are these grades set? Are you trying to live up to someone else's expectations of you, or are you simply trying to please others? You may have set your own standards, but your standards may be so high that they are unattainable, and perhaps by not being so hard on yourself, things may become easier and more enjoyable.

Yes, I think we need to strive to be successful if that is what we want but, I think we should be realistic in how we measure success, because achieving something small by doing something well can be counted as a success, and being successful doesn't mean that you have to be first in everything, or at the top or have the most possessions and money.

Maybe what you should be measuring is how much pleasure you are getting from life and that means pleasing yourself. If you are not getting pleasure from what you are doing then actually you are hindering the process of living your life as you should, and perhaps what you are doing is living the life that you feel is expected of you. People have different ideas on what "success" is, but as long as you are happy and trying to do the best that you can, in what ever you want to succeed in, then you will. Working towards being successful gives you a sense of purpose. Sometimes you may fail and I would like you to say to yourself that "Yes, it is OK to fail sometimes, and I give myself permission to fail (if it happens)". It is not unusual to fail as others do sometimes. What you are actually doing is learning. Each process that you go through, to get to where you want to be in life, you will have learnt something so don't be afraid to fail, learn from it and try again. Learning is really a valuable lesson

Success starts from a seed within. It could be an idea, a goal, a want, a desire but what we think we should be doing to achieve it sometimes gives us such stress. Stress can make us ill, but sometimes people feel that if they are not stressed, then they are not working harder enough – wrong. If we can learn to relax more, we actually achieve more. Running around 'like a headless chicken' is such a waste of valuable time and if we can learn to structure our working life and our leisure time to the best advantage, then we can feel relaxed which actually creates clearer thoughts. Then the stress will start to lift off your shoulders. Saying no occasionally can actually be life changing and can make you feel more chilled. Sometimes doing something tomorrow can make all the difference. It can take the pressure off and because you will have clearer thoughts, it will be easier!

Wow, wouldn't that be lovely to feel like that, and why shouldn't you? We cannot all be perfect and what is perfect anyway? Is it what you think you should be, or is it how other people think you should be? Two very different questions, and when you start to think about them, then maybe you will not feel guilty if you do not always live up to a certain standard, either yours or others. Once you understand that there is no right or wrong way to go about being successful, then there is no limit to the success you can have. Once you realise that your idea of success may not be other peoples, then you can move on and actually be more successful in whatever you want or are doing.

You are a success at whatever you are doing right now.

Never be judgmental of others' success, if you feel they may be more successful than you, they may actually be thinking the same about you. They may be wishing they could do something that you do, and in their eyes you could be more successful than they think they are themselves.

Possibly it's how we think that puts limitations on what we can achieve, so we should stop being self-critical. You are you, so if you find yourself putting yourself down sometimes, start praising yourself for what you have achieved, then you can start moving to where ever it is that you want to be. Success really is only in the mind. Change possibly the way you perceive yourself, and others, and try not to measure success by how much money you have.

MONEY

It can buy a house - but never a home
It can buy a clock - but not time
It can buy you a position - but not respect
It can buy a bed - but not sleep
It can buy you a book - but not knowledge
It can buy you medicines - but not health
It can buy you acquaintances - but never friends
It can buy you blood - but not life
It can buy you sex – but not love

Chapter 12
Beliefs...My angels

Treat the other man's faith gently; it is all he has to believe with.
His mind was created for his own thoughts – not yours or mine
Henry S Haskins

This section may not be for everyone – it is about my faith and my finding spiritualism which is now playing a big part in my life. It is also a big part of many other people's lives and you either choose to believe, or not; that is up to the individual. I do not want to get in to a debate about this, as this is not the point of this book, but what I would like to say is that no matter what gender, race or belief system you follow, to me is not important. I think 'a believe' in itself far outweighs who is right and who is wrong. It really does not matter. But if you do not believe in anything then that is also OK.

Spiritualism came into my life quite late and I can only imagine that to be without my belief now would be unbearable. When my eyes were opened and I was receptive to 'my angels', and 'spirit guides' then I began to see everything in full colour and not black. When I used to shut my eyes, all I saw was black and darkness - most people do - as that is what they expect to see. But once I opened up to a belief, then my life became full of colour when I both shut my eyes and opened them - I would hate to go back to the darkness. It has opened up a whole new world for me. I also believe that you don't have to go to a place of worship to be spiritual. You can practice this where ever you are, and in what ever you are doing.

Every spiritual experience that I have written about in my letter has been an amazing gradual journey which has got stronger and stronger as time has gone on and I have become more open. It has also given me more of an understanding about life and the more I have read and learnt, it has strengthened my belief and helped me to look at life in a different way. I am beginning to understand more about what our lives are about, and why we are here to learn some of the lessons we may have to go through. It has given me a very peaceful feeling but I still have an amazing amount to learn.

So let me explain as it has been a gradual journey and at first in some ways I knew so little. I felt that in my times of trouble that someone or something was looking after me, although I was not sure in the beginning who or what that was. But I learnt very early on that it was OK to 'trust' and the pictures and information that I was receiving were so beautiful, that I could not ignore them, nor did I want to. I think the overriding factor for me was that they showed me I was not on my own anymore; 'they' were my support, and guidance.

What I do know is that I have been blessed, for whatever reason to be able to see and hear my spirit guides. As I have tried to explain in 'my letter' they have spoken to me – but, peculiarly, in only one ear - my angels have cuddled me and been with me always (although I hadn't realised it at the beginning). My mum and dad (both deceased) have both shown themselves to me in different ways, and I have not imagined any of it. Sometimes at the beginning I used to question what I have seen or heard, and then I think to myself - if I was spoken to, I would hear normal speech in both ears, but this has always been in one ear only, and there is no way in a thousand years that I could have created the pictures I have seen. It is sometimes like having a cinema or TV screen all to myself. It is truly amazing I can assure you, but I cannot begin to understand how it happens. I just let it happen as it is so beautiful and seriously, words cannot describe it.

Also, I often find myself saying words that I have no idea what I am actually saying, and cannot remember afterwards, but they come out of my mouth often to help the person that I am speaking to. Where they come from I am not sure, but, trust me, they do have amazing results. The words I speak are often what people need to hear for a number of reasons. Sometimes it is to help them move on, other times it is to help them look at themselves in a new way, other times it is a comfort. But, for whatever reason, I just accept that I say these words when prompted, and so many people over the years have said "thank you, you helped me so much" which is very special to me. This can happen when speaking to someone in a normal conversation or sometimes I do 'angel card' readings with people. This is similar to a tarot card reading where your future opportunities may be revealed but with angel cards this is more about the person themselves.

I feel very privileged to have had the chance for my eyes to be opened, and to feel that I am being looked after, every step of the way, and also to have helped others. We all, every single one of us, has a guardian angel who is always with us by our side, and is never judgmental. Just think of how many times in music, in paintings and literature, angels are mentioned. There are so many songs in the charts, old and new, that talk about spirituality and angels that I know a lot of people are opening their eyes, and want to learn more.

Maybe this is because there is a big 'shift' in the earth's energy, as we are coming into 'The Age of Aquarius, the age of individual enlightenment and Brotherhood of Man' which is a time when the mind, body and soul come together and flow with the universal energies.[1]

If you want to open up to your spirituality, then please do so but with care and respect for what you are about to discover. I know there is a culture of young people who are starting to 'open up', so please do take care and do not do anything until you understand what you are doing. I would advise not to just do it for the fun of it. Do it properly, and with guidance and never make light of it, but enjoy the experience.

There are so many 'believers' all over the world, and sometimes the first thing people do, in times of trouble, is pray. Then to me they have to ask themselves "why do I pray?" They may not pray in a place of worship (I don't) but they do 'talk to someone'. Who is it they talk to and why? But, of course, there are those who ask "if there is a God, then why has this or that been allowed to happen?" I do not fully understand why some people catch fatal diseases or huge disasters in the world happen. There are possibly many different reasons and I am beginning to understand some of them more now through reading and learning but that's a whole different subject and not one to be debated here.

I have had quite a few discussions with friends over the years who say to me "give me some proof there are angels and spirit guides," but I can't. And because it is only I who have seen and felt and heard my own angels, spirit guides and my mum and dad, then however hard I try to tell them, because they are non-believers, I cannot prove anything as I do not have a scientific mind (or the apparatus) to set about proving it. Put it another way though, prove to me why they should not exist?

If you do not 'believe' in anything, then that is fine, everyone has a choice and it is not the purpose of this book to change your beliefs; that is up to you. There are some sceptics who have been converted through making their own scientific studies.

Many Lives, Many Masters written by Dr. Brian Weiss, who is a leading American physician; psychiatrist and sceptic had his whole life changed by certain spiritual experiences. It is a true story. He was worried to say anything in case his scientific colleagues would laugh at him, so it took him four years to complete the book, but he knew he had to write it as he now had the facts in front of him, which is what the scientists want. The interesting part to this true story is there were a lot of other people, and some were Dr Weiss' colleagues, who had seen or felt spiritual experiences but were too afraid to say, in case they were laughed at but they knew that they had occurred! He has since written many others books, and grown more spiritual himself-and he is a scientist!

If you are a sceptic, or would like to learn more, please do read this book as I think you will find it fascinating. There are many other books on this subject as well.

In a similar way, my eyes were opened twenty years ago, when I went to see a homeopathic doctor for my daughter, because she was suffering from epilepsy. He gave her some tablets, which contained Deadly Nightshade. I was horrified and of course questioned him. He said to me "why do you think it was put on this earth, along with stinging nettles, etc?" Now I realise as do many others that many of our medicines and cures can be found in nature, and in particular, the rain forests. So, who created them in the first place? As the doctor said, "why are they there?" Good question I think. They must have come from somewhere

Actually, we all do have the ability to tap into our own powers, and a lot of you have already done so, without realising that you have. How many of you actually do know that something is going to happen, or see something which you do not understand, but later it transpires into reality? You may have had a recollection that you have been somewhere before. Have you ever followed your 'gut instinct'? These are all connected to your spiritual awareness, but you may not call them that, and it is up to you if you want to develop this further, or just dismiss it.

Another aspect of your spiritual awareness that you may not have realised is we all, whether you like it or not or believe it or not, have our own guardian angel. Sometimes we can feel her, or him, and often they come to you in different ways. To give you an example; have you ever had something that you wanted to know, or had something bothering you? Suddenly an idea popped into your head which resolved the problem. Where did that idea suddenly come from? Have you ever been drawn into a book shop and just the right book has jumped off the shelf, and is exactly what you wanted to know or learn. Well, possibly that thought to go into that bookshop might have come from your angel, don't you think? Where else did it come from? Or you may have been drawn towards someone who can help you solve a problem, and you may not have known them before. People have been saved when someone mysteriously appeared from nowhere to come to their rescue in their exact time of need. I really could list a whole number of examples where angels appear, and if anyone of you wants to draw your angel close to you, you only have to ask.

They can be more obvious in your life if you allow them to be. They can hear what your thoughts are; they can help you in ways that you never dreamed of. I am not saying that you will feel or see them as I have, but, they are there waiting for you to ask. There are some beautiful books which can help you learn how to do this. Or type in 'angels' on the internet and see how many wonderful sites you will find.[5]

Having angels in my life has been so wonderful, that I would hate to have a life without them now. Oh, you may laugh and think I am stupid, but really in some ways I do not care, as to me they are part of my life now, and I love every minute of it. It has lead to peace within me, and that is so very lovely. I am sure it will help lead you there as well, being at peace with yourself, if you want! But, most importantly just knowing that 'they' are there for you is the first step, and if you want to learn more, you know what to do! Just ask.

Activity

Catch the thoughts that whisper in your mind

Just ask... by making a little time for yourself. Sit quietly, relax as much as possible and shut your eyes. Perhaps turn on some relaxing light music, or light some candles. Let your mind go as blank as you can. If your mind will not sit still, a good way of pushing away all the things that may pop into your head is to try if you can to concentrate on your breathing by listening to its flow.

Learn to play about with your breaths and this will relax your mind. Count your number of breaths, try and make them go really slowly and feel your chest rising and falling rhythmically. Play around with your breathing for a while, and see what happens. Also try and let the rest of your body relax from your head right down to your toes. The more you practice this the easier it becomes

If you can do a meditation, even better, but you don't have to. If you find that you cannot do this, then at any time, start to talk to your angel and spirit guide, quietly and gently in your mind, at what ever time of day you feel you can and need to. You see, he/she will be listening even if you don't realise it or feel anything at that moment. But catch those thoughts that whispered in your mind

Or, you may be surprised later when you least expect it. Keep doing this as often as you can, and who knows, you may find yourself wanting to learn more, or feeling more at peace with yourself which is the nicest feeling you can give yourself. If you have no desire to change your beliefs, or anything in your life, 'they' understand as well as we all have freedom of choice.

The whole object of this book is for you understand that you can have such a wonderful life if you want to. You do not have to believe in angels, but you have to believe in yourself. By believing in yourself, and following your dreams, you can get to a stage where you can learn that some things in life happen for a reason, and if you learn from that reason, you can move mountains. The struggle will be over. Or you can choose to stay exactly where you are now. The choice is yours.

Chapter 13
Make it happen

Your thoughts become your words,
Your words become your actions,
Your actions become your habits
Your habits become your character,
Your character becomes your destiny
Unknown

Much has been written in this book about my life and about my thoughts on life, and I firmly believe that you, and only you, can make a difference to your life if you are prepared to try and change (if you need to). It is easy to read about other people achieving all sorts of things and to be inspired by them, but you too can grab the opportunities presented to you if your mind is ready and willing to recognise them; you too can accept challenges if you are willing to try something new and to test yourself in what you can achieve. But nothing much will happen unless you do something to make it happen. So before you put this book down you might like to make a note of these twelve points. ......practise doing what the words say and maybe take a saying each day over the next couple of weeks or, perhaps take one saying a month, and practise and interpret into actions what the words mean to you...... and be conscious of what effect your actions have on yourself and others.

1. Believe in yourself
2. Look for new opportunities
3. Be committed and focused
4. Love and really enjoy what you have
5. Decide to take charge of your own life
6. Know that you are strong – you will survive
7. Be honest with yourself and truthful to others
8. Trust your heart
9. Turn your inspirations into reality
10. Stop being a victim by letting go
11. Trust that you are in the right place at the right time
12. Believe in your own power and never give it away

Here also are some simple ideas to put a sparkle back into your eyes

Help someone once a day – it will give you both pleasure
Smile more often – notice how you feel
Compliment someone
Laugh often – even over silly things
Do something spontaneous and give someone a surprise
Make some time for yourself at least once a day/week
Do something you have never done before – try
something new
Do an activity once a week like sing (even in the bath),
dance, listen to music etc
Be passionate about something
Give someone a hug
Say those three little words – you're loved ones cannot
read your mind!
Spend one hour a day really talking and listening to
someone
Share your family meals around a table as often as you
can
Make a commitment to have friends round for dinner once
a week
Explore nature – the woods, rivers, ponds and plants
– take a walk
Be aware of your day –good and bad

Shout to others about something good you have done or achieved
Praise others more – especially children
Cut your television viewing down by half
Count your blessings and appreciate what you have
– they may disappear one day!
Live in the NOW and not in the past
Don't regret anything
Make that phone call – it only takes a few minutes
Don't say "When I have ......" why would this make you happy?
Happiness comes from within – not material possessions
Flow with the tide, rather than against it.
And be proud to be you – you are unique

Chapter 14
Something to think about!

Life is no brief candle to me. It is a sort of splendid torch which I have got a hold of for the moment, and I want to make it burn as brightly as possible before handing it on to future generations
— George Bernard Shaw — Writer 1856-1950

Celebration of life

Now, you can shut this book and put it on the bookshelf, or you can read on as I would like you to think about something. Something which will only take a minute to read, but it may have a big impact on you.

Why do we as a culture wait until people die before we tell them how much we love them in our prayers or through talking silently to them in our minds? Why do we wait to say how much they mean to us until they cannot hear us? Why do we wait until it is too late before we recall their good qualities? What good does it do then?

Why don't we do it now, so that the person can hear, feel and enjoy the love that we have for them? Wouldn't it be nicer for that person to know that they are 'special' to you, and for them to know that they have made a difference in your life, and how much you appreciate them? Think of the loss and emptiness you would feel if they were not there, and you had not said those three little words, which mean so much. ..I love you.

Wouldn't it be nice if you could start to tell the people that are around you, how much they mean to you, and how much you appreciate them in your life? Your partner, parents, friends and children don't always 'know' how you feel, so why assume that they do? They can't read your mind, and however much you love someone in your thoughts, actions really do speak louder than words.

Activity

This will only take a few minutes to do, but it could make so much difference to you and others

Do you love someone? Then perhaps you could tell them, and give them a hug
Has someone been an influence or made a difference in your life, then why not give them a call?

Let the friends in your life know what a big impact they have had on you, and how much you appreciate their friendships.

Or maybe write someone a letter or send a card and tell them if you find it hard to express your feeling.
There is sometimes something special about a card or letter that expresses love or feelings; it can say so much (and it's so easy with e-mail, too)

Life is too short to leave kind words unsaid. The words you say, the action that you may take, or the letter you may write, might just make all the difference in the world, and costs very little if at all, but lasts forever.

There is also something else you could do but this will take longer -

Activity

Your family may like to know, before it is too late, some of the things that have been important to you. Write a letter to your own family about your life, so that one day, or now, your family can read it and remember you how you would like them to.

What would you like to be remembered for, and is there anything that you would like to say to them? Express how you feel and what you have achieved. Maybe you would like them to read it now, while you are alive, or you may want to keep it a secret. It really does not matter.

It doesn't have to be long, but I am sure they will cherish it, and may read it often.

(Please also see end page for other ways of writing your life story which you may find easier)

I came across these little thoughts that I would like to end with as I think they say it all.

People come into your life for a reason

People come into your life for a reason, a season, or a lifetime. When you figure out which it is, you know exactly what to do.

When someone is in your life for a REASON, it is usually to meet a need you have expressed outwardly or inwardly. They have come to assist you through a difficulty, to provide you with guidance and support, to aid you physically, emotionally or spiritually.

They may seem like a godsend - which they are. They are there for the reason you need them to be. Then, without any wrongdoing on your part or at an inconvenient time, this person will say or do something to bring the relationship to an end. Sometimes they die. Sometimes they walk away. Sometimes they act up or out and force you to take a stand.

What we must realise is that once our need has been met, our desire fulfilled, their work is done. The prayer you sent up has been answered and it is then time for you and them to move on.

When people come into your life for a SEASON, it is because your turn has come to share, grow or learn. They may bring you an experience of peace or make you laugh. They may teach you something you have never known or done. They usually give you an unbelievable amount of joy. Believe it! It is real! But only for a season.

LIFETIME relationships teach you lifetime lessons: those things you must build upon in order to have a solid emotional foundation.

Your job is to accept the lesson. Love the person or people in question (in the way that is right for them) and put what you have learned to use in all other relationships and areas of your life.

It is said that love is blind, but friendships are forever. Thank you for being part of my life......

FOOTPRINTS

One night I had a dream

I dreamed that I was walking along the beach with God and across the sky flashed scenes from my life.

For each scene I noticed two sets of footprints in the sand, one belonged to me and the other to God.

When the last scene of my life flashed before me I looked back at the footprints in the sand.

I noticed that at times along the path of life there were only one set of footprints.

I also noticed that it happened at the very lowest and saddest times in my life.

This really bothered me and I questioned God about it.

"God, You said that once I decided to follow you, You would walk with me all the way but I noticed that during the most troublesome time of my life, there is only one set of footprints

I don't understand why in times when I needed You most, You would leave me"

God replied, "My precious child, I love you and I would never leave you during your times of trials and suffering.

When you saw only one set of footprints it was then that I carried you"

ANON

A lovely poem that was sent to me by my editor

Letter to my children

Thank you for the love you give
And all the joy you've brought
For all the times when you were small
And filled each waking thought
For all the laughter, smiles and tears
The studying and stress
The memory of muddy boots
That special party dress

The days the house filled up with friends
I never knew each name
The growing up, the leaving home
How quiet life became
The letters, cards and photographs
Each play their special part
But thank you for the love we share
Still growing in my heart

Iris Hesselden

This I saw on the internet just after September 11th 2001

May today there be peace within you. May you trust God that you are exactly where you are meant to be. "I believe that friends are quiet angels who lift us to our feet when our wings have trouble remembering how to fly."

Suggested reading

I have found a lot of inspiration from some of the books I have read over the years and I list below a few that you may like to read. Most of these authors have written other books which you may find interesting.

Weekend Life Coach by Lynda Field and published by Vermillion.

Create Your Own Future by Linda Georgian and published by Simon and Schuster.

The Power is Within You by Louise L. Hay and published by Hay House.

The Road Less Travelled by M. Scott Peck and published by Arrow.

Messengers of Light by Terry Lynn Taylor and published by H. J. Kramer Inc.

Ask Your Angels by Alma Daniel, Timothy Wyllie and Andrew Ramer and published by Piatkus.

Opening To Channel by Sanaya Roman and Duanne Packer and published by H. J. Kramer Inc.

Many lives, Many Masters by Dr. Brian Weiss and published by Piatkus.

Messages from the Masters by Dr Brian Weiss and published by Piatkus

From Strength to Strength by Sara Henderson and published by Pan Macmillan.

Some books I have come across which you may like to fill in yourself for your children and grandchildren to read about your life. The Grandparent book ISBN 1856451429 or My Life Has a Story written by Amy Brennan published by Authorhouse. I am sure there are many others books available

I also found two wonderful websites which you may like to visit if you would like to know more about *The Universe and Spiritualism*. http://www.crystallotus.com and http://www.crystalinks.com. Both highly informative.

Your library or local bookstore may have other books that you would find helpful.

Happy reading.

End Notes

[1] The Age of Aquarius simply means we are leaving one age Pisces (the fish) and entering into a new one Aquarius (the water bearer) and this happens every two thousand years. This New Age comes about through a spontaneous raising of consciousness of the whole planet. We have seen evidence of this perhaps, with the death of Princess Diana and the act of terrorism in New York on 9/11/01 – the outrage and the depth of feeling felt and expressed the world over. However, on the opposite side of the coin, others believe that astrology is a massive deception website address http://www.ajco.demon.co.uk/acquarius

[2] The British Epilepsy Association – for further advise and help please call their helpline telephone 0808 800 5050

[3] The Dyslexia Institute – for further advise and information please call their Head Office on 01784 222300

British Dyslexia Association – for further advise and information, please call their helpline on 0118 9668271

[4] Grandparents' Association – for further information please write to them at: Moot House, The Stow, Harlow, Essex CM20 3AG or their help line telephone number is 0845 434 9585. Website http://www.grandparents-association.org.uk

[5] Two websites that you may find interesting http://www.crystallotus.com and http://www.crystalinks.com

If you would like to become a Volunteer or would like further information from Victim Support – their National Office telephone number is 0207 735 9166 or visit their website http://www.victimsupport.org